Y0-DYH-673

Written Expression: The Principal's Survival Guide

India Podsen
Charles Allen
Glenn Pethel
John Waide

EYE ON EDUCATION
6 Depot Way West, Suite 106
Larchmont, NY 10538
(914) 833-0551
(914) 833-0761 fax

Library of Congress Cataloging-in-Publication Data

Written expression : the principal's survival guide / India Podsen ... [et al.].
p. cm. -- (School leadership library)
Includes bibliographical references.
ISBN 1-883001-34-X
1. Authorship--Handbooks, manuals, etc. 2. School administrators--Handbooks, manuals, etc. I. Podsen, India, 1945- . II. Series.
PN145.W78 1997
808'.042'024371--dc21 96-40532
CIP

10 9 8 7 6 5 4 3 2 1

Production services provided by William Bragg, P.O. Box 1562, Fort Lee, NJ 07024 (201-947-1749)

Published by Eye On Education

DISK WITH WORKBOOK TO ACCOMPANY WRITTEN EXPRESSION: The Principal's Survival Guide
By India Podsen

INSTRUCTION AND THE LEARNING ENVIRONMENT
By James Keefe and John Jenkins

RESOURCE ALLOCATION: Managing Money and People
By M. Scott Norton and Larry K. Kelly

ORGANIZATIONAL OVERSIGHT: Planning and Scheduling for Effectiveness
By David A. Erlandson, Peggy L. Stark, and Sharon M. Ward

MOTIVATING OTHERS: Creating the Conditions
By David P. Thompson

INTERPERSONAL SENSITIVITY
By John R. Hoyle and Harrison M. Crenshaw

ORAL AND NONVERBAL EXPRESSION
By Ivan Muse

LEADERSHIP: A Relevant a Realistic Role for Principals
By Gary Crow, Joseph Matthews, and Lloyd McCleary

JUDGMENT: Making the Right Calls
By Jim Sweeney and Diana Bourisaw

PROBLEM ANALYSIS: Responding to School Complexity
By Charles M. Achilles, John S. Reynolds, and Susan H. Achilles

THE REFLECTIVE SUPERVISOR: A Practical Guide For Educators
By Ray Calabrese and Sally Zepeda

HANDS-ON LEADERSHIP TOOLS FOR PRINCIPALS
By Ray Calabrese, Gary Short, and Sally Zepeda

LEADERSHIP THROUGH COLLABORATION: Alternatives to the Hierarchy
By Michael Koehler and Jeanne C. Baxter

HUMAN RESOURCES ADMINISTRATION: A School Based Perspective
By Richard E. Smith

THE PRINCIPAL AS STEWARD
By Jack McCall

THE PRINCIPAL'S EDGE
By Jack McCall

About the Authors

India J. Podsen is Associate Professor of Middle/Secondary Education at North Georgia College and State University in Dahlonega, Georgia. Prior to this position she co-directed and then directed the Principal's Center at Georgia State University in Atlanta for ten years. This book grew out of Podsen's 25 years of professional experiences as an English teacher, school administrator, staff developer in leadership training, assessment center director and consultant to the National Association of Secondary School Principals (NASSP).

Charles Allen is an education consultant and former Director of the Maryland Assessment and Leadership Training Center. He has taught English at the middle/high school levels and has served as a school principal and central office assistant superintendent.

Glenn Pethel works in the Gwinnett County (Georgia) Public Schools as the Executive Director for Human Resources. He also has experience as a teacher, school administrator and university instructor, and conducts seminars and workshops on a variety of school related topics, including effective communication.

John Waide, a former educational administrator, currently consults with school districts in conducting leadership workshops in such areas as time management, educational technology, goal setting, and effective writing.

Foreword

The School Leadership Library was designed to show practicing and aspiring principals what they should know and be able to do to be effective leaders of their schools. The books in this series were written to answer the question, "How can we improve our schools by improving the effectiveness of our principals?"

Success in the principalship, like in other professions, requires mastery of a knowledge and skills base. One of the goals of the National Policy Board for Educational Administration (sponsored by NAESP, NASSP, AASA, ASCD, NCPEA, UCEA, and other professional organizations) was to define and organize that knowledge and skill base. The result of our efforts was the development of a set of 21 "domains," building blocks representing the core understanding and capabilities required of successful principals.

The 21 domains of knowledge and skills are organized under four broad areas: Functional, Programmatic, Interpersonal, and Contextual. They are as follows:

FUNCTIONAL DOMAINS
- Leadership
- Information Collection
- Problem Analysis
- Judgment
- Organizational Oversight
- Implementation
- Delegation

INTERPERSONAL DOMAINS
- Motivating Others
- Interpersonal Sensitivity
- Oral and Nonverbal Expression
- Written Expression

PROGRAMMATIC DOMAINS
- Instruction and the Learning Environment
- Curriculum Design
- Student Guidance and Development
- Staff Development
- Measurement and Evaluation
- Resource Allocation

CONTEXTUAL DOMAINS
- Philosophical and Cultural Values
- Legal and Regulatory Applications
- Policy and Political Influences
- Public Relations

These domains are not discrete, separate entities. Rather, they evolved only for the purpose of providing manageable descriptions of essential content and practice so as to better understand the entire complex role of the principalship. Because human behavior comes in "bunches" rather than neat packages, they are also overlapping pieces of a complex puzzle. Consider the domains as converging streams of behavior that spill over one another's banks but that all contribute to the total reservoir of knowledge and skills required of today's principals.

The School Leadership Library was established by General Editors David Erlandson and Al Wilson to provide a broad examination of the content and skills in all of the domains. The authors of each volume in this series offer concrete and realistic illustrations and examples, along with reflective exercises. You will find their work to be of exceptional merit, illustrating with insight the depth and interconnectedness of the domains. This series provides the fullest, most contemporary, and most useful information available for the preparation and professional development of principals.

Scott Thomson, Executive Secretary
National Policy Board for Educational Administration

If you would like information about how to become a member of the **School Leadership Library,** please contact

Eye On Education
6 Depot Way West, Suite 106
Larchmont, NY 10538
(914) 833-0551 (914) 833-0761 FAX

PREFACE

Principals must write often in the daily performance of their jobs, and they must write effectively if they are to perform their jobs effectively. Schools are human organizations and, like other human organizations, they are held together by communication. Schools are also complex organizations and they exist in complex human environments. As a result, the communications that link the parts must be precise, timely, and sensitive to the various audiences that comprise the school and its environment. The principal must become a master not only of the mechanics of written communications, but of the nuances of expression that are captured and recorded in the written messages that he or she sends.

Written communication is bound by a somewhat different set of conventions and rules than those that apply to oral communication. The clever conversationalist or public speaker can readily assess misunderstanding, confusion, or hostility in his or her audience and can make quick adjustments to reshape the communication to make it more effective. The writer does not have the same advantage. Once a written message is sent, it remains as an artifact of the writer's intent, to be examined and re-examined at the audience's pleasure. Corrections to faulty written communications are usually difficult to make and generally not very timely. Written communication needs to get it right the first time.

Furthermore, because the different school audiences are different in their expectations for the school and because they seldom are in the same place at the same time, oral communication channels are not sufficient to handle the messages that must flow among the human elements that exist in the school and its environment. For example, how often does a principal have the opportunity to send out a single oral message to all the school's parents? Much communication with this group will necessarily be in written form. Nor are oral communications likely to be sufficient even for audiences internal to the school, i.e., students and teachers. Written announcements and memos will play an important part of the school's internal communication.

Also, the principal must remember that these audiences are different. The principal cannot send out a single memorandum to staff, students, parents, and superintendent. Nor are the same style and language appropriate with these different audiences. Each of these audiences is interested in a school event or program for different reasons; each will participate and provide support in a different way. Special written communications, in one form or another, are required for each of these audiences, and these communications must be in language that the members of the audience can understand, that is consistent with their legitimate expectations for the school, and is sensitive to their expectations and needs. Meeting these standards is no small task. Yet the principal's survival and success in providing for leadership for the school is, in no small measure, dependent upon his or her ability to do so.

India Posden, Charles Allen, Glenn Pethel, and John Waide have assembled this volume, *Written Expression: The Principal's Survival Guide,* with the principal's needs in mind. While they recognize that all principals face similar challenges in written communications with their varying audiences, they also recognize that all principals have different backgrounds and different skill levels as they attempt to consistently create and transmit effective written documents for their various audiences. They provide numerous examples of good written communication, numerous practice exercises for the principal, and numerous opportunities for the reader to assess and improve his or her own effectiveness in written expression.

Throughout the books the comprise the *School Leadership Library,* it is emphasized that the principal cannot lead the school alone. The active support of all persons and groups in the school and the larger community must be solicited and harnessed in support of the task of educating society's youth for a better future. This active support can only be enlisted, coordinated, and maintained if the written communications that come out of the principal's office consistently send, through divergent channels, an effective unifying message about the purpose of the school and the steps that must be taken to accomplish it.

David A. Erlandson
Alfred P. Wilson

TABLE OF CONTENTS

Acknowledgements

This book reflects the work, concern, and support of many people who care about principals and the quality of their performance in our schools.

Thanks to Dr. Dave Erlandson who gave me the opportunity to tackle this project; to my co-authors who provided immense support and friendship; and to the principals who contributed their correspondence files for job writing samples: Dr. Kathleen Semergieff, Dr. Catherine Hackney, Mr. Nicholas Rizzo, Mr. Ronald Vale, Mr. Joseph Hayward, Mr. Max Mc Millan, and Dr. James LoFrese.

Thanks also to the computer geniuses who invented personal computers and the wonderful software programs that constantly challenged my technological skills. Here a special thanks goes to my husband, Hank Podsen, for his expertise in unraveling computer glitches, keeping me sane, and supporting my professional endeavors.

But perhaps most of all, thanks to my professional mentors who have cleared the path for me and made this all possible. Paul Hersey and Ray Lemley who gave me the chance to work with NASSP's *From the Desk of...;* Scott Thomson who provided the opportunity to work with the National Policy Board in its efforts to design a core curriculum for school administrators; and Joe Richardson who gave me the opportunity to work with him in directing the Principals Center.

Part One

Challenging the Status Quo

Year 2000 and Beyond: New Century and New Challenges

As we approach the twenty-first century, it is essential to take a fresh look at our relationship to teachers, students, parents, the local community, our profession, and the way we manage our workplace. The current decade, born of the almost overwhelming social, political, and technological changes of the '70s and the '80s, already demonstrates a unique dynamic with important implications for our professional and personal success.

Uncertainty Factors

As a school principal you first need to be aware of the many uncertainties that will powerfully influence school tactics and outcomes. To navigate through the shifting sands that lie ahead, you must learn more sophisticated strategic game plans. The broad generalizations that satisfied school communities in the past are not sufficient guidance for today's educational consumers.

Without doubt, we will continue to experience the tug-of-war interplay of national and global forces that can redefine entire school cultures virtually overnight. In response to approximately 120 national reform reports, educators and politicians acted around the country. Their actions resulted in such things as:

- Changes in standards for teacher certification
- Emphasis on education for cultural diversity
- Financial rewards for schools that show significant increases on standardized tests
- Increased involvement of parents in children's education
- Increased requirements for high school graduation

The list goes on. The point is this: Global politics will continue to set in place both competitive and protectionist movements that challenge old ways of doing business. How we respond to these movements will have major consequences on our schools. Keeping up with and managing these movements will require strong ongoing education and training for all professional educators.

TECH WAVES

The demand for knowledge and skills is never-ending. Tech-knowledge is required even for those of us who aren't tech experts. Jackson (1990) tells us that if you don't know how to put it together, you must certainly know how to put it to use. With the rapid expansion of data bases and information systems, it's probably even more important to learn how to deal with what's new. Things will surface by this time next year that we can't imagine today. As we close out the twentieth century new ways of thinking about knowledge are changing; the learning lines are merging between and among a multitude of previously separate disciplines. Lifetime learning is here to stay. What does this mean to you and your school?

THE PRINCIPAL AS ENTREPRENEUR

The entrepreneurial perspective is a significant force in our work history. With discussions of choice and school vouchers in many school board meetings, principals may need to consider marketing their schools in ways (more use of multimedia and interactive technologies) that highlight specific instructional programs, accomplishments, and achievements. The emphasis today is on results. Given the dynamics of this explosive new age we work in, it is almost inevitable that the accountability factor is here to stay. George Pawlas (1995) in his text, *The Administrator's Guide to School Community Relations*, emphasizes this saying, "Today is the day and age of accountability, and that accountability is built into the jobs of educational administrators" (p 2).

SO WHAT DOES THIS HAVE TO DO WITH WRITTEN EXPRESSION?

We mentioned earlier that it is important for principals to take a fresh look at their relationship with staff, students, parents, and the local community. It's time to take a hard look at the way we conduct school business.

One performance area that impacts on our ability to manage schools is our capability to communicate effectively. Written expression is a skill area that any educator would readily agree is *crucial* to job success, but research in adult writing skills indicates that this adeptness is not steadily developed once an individual graduates from college (Aldrich, 1982). As community and instructional leaders, principals have the opportunity both to model and to teach the power of the written word. This domain focuses on ways to help professionals fine-tune and master this essential craft: how to organize thoughts logically and succinctly, choose appropriate formats for written documents, and reach targeted audiences. More important, writing well is a skill that our school community expects us to demonstrate at a high level of proficiency. Today, it is more than expected; it is demanded.

HOW TO USE THIS GUIDE

In researching information for this book, we asked school principals two questions: "Why would you use a guide on written expression?" and "What would you find helpful?"

In response to the first question, principals said that they would go to a reference guide on written communication because they were experiencing a particular problem either with a specific audience or with a type of writing. With this in mind, we decided to develop a guide that addresses the audiences principals communicate with most often. While all of our written communication usually concerns students directly or indirectly, we decided not to include this group since the majority of administrative writing goes to staff, parents and the central office, your primary audiences. Your secondary audiences include your peers, the local community, and your professional colleagues. These are presented by order of contact frequency.

In response to the second question, principals emphasized that a guide on written communication should be "user friendly." Time is a critical factor. The reference guide should provide suggestions which are quick and easy to follow. In keeping with this advice, we took the "what you need to know approach." We present key information and ways for you to resolve the problem situation you are experiencing. We do not pretend that we have covered the topic comprehensively; rather we try to provide the most current and relevant resources for you to explore if you need further information and decide to investigate an area more thoroughly.

Moreover, we wanted to develop a guide that was interactive and stimulated you to think about written expression in a reflective manner. To accomplish this goal, we offer numerous exercises encouraging you to self-assess yourself and your school. For those of you seeking more practice, we offer *Disk with Workbook to Accompany Written Expression: The Principal's Survival Guide* which presents the types of writing most often used by principals on the job. Each type is preceded by a brief summary of the best practices and followed, when feasible, by examples written by school administrators. A document analysis which highlights the effective strategies demonstrated by the writer accompanies each sample. The purpose of these examples is to assist you in building a wide repertoire of writing strategies for use on the job.

On the diskette, you will find many of the sample documents printed in both this book and the workbook. You may use these documents as templates for your own writing tasks.

In summary, *Written Expression: The Principal's Survival Guide* is just what the name implies—a reference guide for school administrators on the subject of job writing. We hope it helps you to sharpen your professional image and make the job of writing easier and more enjoyable.

1

Fostering Open Communication

"If we keep on doing what we've been doing, then we will keep getting the same thing we've been getting."
—Anonymous

Why is This Important? What's the Payoff for Me and My School?

When was the last time you assessed your communication effectiveness within your school community? What exactly is the purpose of your written communication? Have you really thought about it? Is it just to provide information about your school, staff, and students, or should it relate to a larger goal?

If your administrative experiences are similar to ours, you probably never really addressed this area in any systematic fashion. As a new administrator the first priority is survival; your main focus is on students, teachers, and the instructional program. Keeping up with and putting out the fires occupies your day. As an experienced professional the day's events have been routinized. Nothing appears to be broken so why tinker with it. Besides, who has the time? Business as usual?

We would ask you to take the time now to reflect on **how** and **why** you do what you do; particularly on how and why you communicate within your school. It's time to take a "fresh look" at your communication agenda. This chapter focuses attention on your communication goals as they relate to your school office, your community relationships, and your methods of collaboration. Each of these aspects relates to building open communication channels in your school.

YOUR COMMUNICATION AGENDA

As a school principal, what is your ultimate communication goal? The purpose of your communication according to Drake and Roe (1994) is "to influence, which implies more thought about your communication than merely throwing out the information for whatever it is worth" to staff, parents and the general community (p. 439).

We believe that the ultimate goal of every school principal is to build trust and solid working relationships with all school related personnel and community members who come in contact with our schools. If you think it is important to be seen as a leader who is committed to sharing information with others and who goes beyond communicating only what is necessary, then this guide will have meaning and value to you.

Developing a climate in which you and your staff are open with information—information exchanges between you and your teachers, between departments or teams, between team members, and between your school and the community—is critical to the success of your school (Conrad, 1985). The essential factor in communication, from our point of view, is professional accountability. *Real communication is being responsible to ensure that a message is received. This means that if the reader doesn't get it, you didn't communicate.*

Generally, most of us approach noncommunication by blaming the other guy, "He never listens," "They never told me." Such common responses deny our answerability in the matter. By being responsible for your communication agenda you create a strategic game plan. You must then discover ways to improve your effectiveness.

Through your writing you demonstrate how you do things in your professional setting. At one level it shows how well (or how poorly) you have mastered written communication—an essential tool for school leaders these days. At another level it is a personal presentation of how you think, and it demonstrates how well you are performing the varied tasks required of a school principal. The bottom line is this. *Your written products assist you in telling your school community what this school is all about, what problems you are facing and resolving, and what results you have achieved.*

Our objective in this chapter is to help you analyze and strengthen your ability to develop and maintain open lines of communication, a key factor in fostering two-way communication systems.

YOUR SCHOOL OFFICE: YOUR COMMUNICATION NERVE CENTER

ALL VISITORS MUST REPORT TO THE MAIN OFFICE

How many times have you seen this sign? Ever thought about changing it? Consider its tone. Does it convey the message you intended?

What impression does your school make on staff, students, parents, and visitors? Have you stepped back from your role as principal to think about this issue? Do you feel it is important enough to spend the time rethinking how you can make this work for you rather than against you as you conduct business? In our current era of accountability can we afford not to think about this matter? For many supporters and critics, is not the *perception* of a situation the *reality* of the situation?

Consider this alternative:

THE SAFETY OF OUR STUDENTS IS MOST IMPORTANT.

ALL VISITORS MUST REPORT TO THE MAIN OFFICE FOR A GUEST PASS

WELCOME TO OUR SCHOOL.

Which sign conveys your intended message? What's the difference in the tone? More important, what impression does each sign have on the reader? Think about it! Which one does a better job and why?

The dictionary defines a nerve as a source from which energy or dynamic action emanates. How energetic or dynamic is your school office? What messages about you, the principal, and about your school are being created and delivered to your various school publics? Your school office staff and their interactions with teachers, students, and parents play a key role in developing open lines of communication.

Let's take a break from the reading to do Exercise 1.1. You are asked to reflect upon your experiences as a school principal and then to interact with colleagues and staff.

Exercise 1.1
SCHOOL OFFICE COMMUNICATIONS INVENTORY

Instructions:

The purpose of this exercise is to help you and your staff assess your interactions with your school audiences.

- STEP ONE: As you read each indicator, write down how you know this descriptor is being performed or not performed. What's your evidence? Describe the quality of that interaction (Good, Acceptable, Marginal, Unknown).
- STEP TWO: Duplicate this form and ask a small group of staff members (certified and non-certified) to record their impressions. Then compare. Ask a small group of parents for their impressions.
- STEP THREE: Visit other schools and assess the impact of the school office. Compare how your school stacks up.

Your Office Staff

- Your office staff greets all visitors and staff courteously and quickly.
- Your office staff tactfully questions callers to determine if the situation requires personal attention of the principal or if another staff member can handle the problem.

- Your office staff has a clear set of duties and responsibilities. These duties and responsibilities are communicated to the entire professional staff both verbally and in written form.
- You assess the training needs of your office staff and provide the necessary staff development. You establish a clear ordering of work priorities.
- Office procedures are established and periodically reviewed with office staff.
- The office staff understands and is committed to the goal of building trust and effective working relationships with all those who interact with the school.

Your Office Environment

- You have assessed your school office layout and design to create a specific impression.
- A professional and attractive waiting area for visitors has been provided.
- Traffic routes have been carefully and functionally developed.
- Both the outer office and your office conveys a businesslike but congenial atmosphere that is conducive to the sharing of information.

Your School/Community Communications

- Your school stationery is attractive and creates a professional image; the quality of the paper enhances the credibility of the sender.
- All general school related documents reflect unity in letterhead design, theme, and color. These documents include report cards, newsletters, flyers, handbooks, memos, sign-in sheets, forms, brochures, business cards, and school stationery, just to name a few.
- All school related documents reflect high quality in format design, accuracy of information, correct grammar, spelling, punctuation, and clarity of purpose.
- Internal communications to staff are systematic. Certain communications are sent at a specific time each day, week or month.

- External communications to students, parents, and peers are routinized. Certain communications are sent at a specific time each day, week, or month.
- Incoming mail and messages are handled with precision. Specific procedures are established to prevent misplacement or loss.
- You have designated an information data base reference area to provide easy access to state department guides, school board policies, personnel policies, operational handbooks, school and community law, and resources on government and social agencies.

However, or whatever you answered above, or even if you didn't answer, thank you for staying with us. You may use as much or as little of this text as you care to or as, in your judgment, you find valuable. We do want you to begin to think about these areas and start conversations with peers, staff, and community members. We do want you to search for pertinent information that will help you to manage and create credible and professional images of you and your school. For more information about designing a productive school office environment, check out Drake and Roe's (1994) chapter entitled, *The School Office: Information and Communication Center.*

CREATING A DYNAMIC FIRST IMPRESSION

Part of creating a dynamic first impression is the ability to meet and greet people in a sincere and helpful way. This comes across in face-to-face interactions and in our writing. Your school secretary and your office staff are the first people parents and teachers meet when they walk into your building. Their work also represents the school in written form.

What tone is set by your office staff? Do they greet visitors quickly and with a smile? Do they help to build a positive school image by making all visitors feel that they are important to this learning community? Or is a parent or student made to feel like an intruder?

What did your communications inventory help you to discover? What are your strength areas? What areas need to be revisited?

Exercise 1.2
School Office Inventory Analysis

	STRENGTHS	GROWTH TARGETS
Office Staff		
Office Environment		
School Communications		

Similarly, what is the impact of your school related written products? Here's a suggestion. Collect every document that you send out through the school office. Arrange them in front of you on a large table. What impression do they create? Here's a checklist to guide your analysis.

Exercise 1.3
Impact Analysis of School Documents

- The documents are visually attractive. The layout draws the reader's attention.
- There is a balance in terms of word text and white space. Pictures, graphic art, tables, or charts are used to support the text when needed.
- The content is accurate in terms of facts and ideas.
- The content readability level is suitable for the intended audience. You have used short words, sentences, and paragraphs.
- The written products are easy to read. The print is sharp and different fonts and sizes are used to enhance readability.
- The written documents are technically correct. There are no typographical errors.
- The school logo or masthead is attention-getting and alerts the reader that this a school communication.
- The school's mission statement is imprinted on the document whenever appropriate.

How many written documents did you review?
What impression are you creating with your readers?

Do you have a systematic approach in communicating school information to staff, parents, and students such as attractive information folders? Is the information easily accessible, or do you send the information home in a blitz of various sizes, shapes, and formats? More important, do they reflect a dynamic school leader who uses every opportunity to make sure that people know what the principal and the school believe is important?

With current computer software and hardware options, we have no excuse in not producing appealing and professional written documents. Your school community not only expects it in today's world but demands it. The quality of these written products conveys as much as the messages they try to get across (Drake and Roe, 1994). What's more, they impact on your professional credibility as a school leader and the credibility of your school as a successful one.

KEEPING THE SCHOOL COMMUNITY INFORMED

As the communications center, the school office receives and sends many written documents. The flow of information within your school setting is essential. To maintain and improve the effectiveness of the school, information must flow systematically upward, laterally, downward, and outward (Conrad, 1985). The following information flow checklist may help you keep in mind the many types of information that should be kept moving (see Figure 1.1).

BUILDING SCHOOL/COMMUNITY RELATIONSHIPS

Communicating only what your various audiences need to know is not communicating enough. According to George Pawlas (1995), principals need to see public relations as one aspect of fostering open communication within the "broader framework of a school/community relations plan." He emphasizes public relations as social accountability. "Social accountability applied to public education means being answerable or accountable to all the publics we serve at our school" (p. 2).

In his text, Pawlas stresses that "many principals confuse school/community relations with public relations...." He argues

FIGURE 1.1. INFORMATION FLOW CHECKLIST

Upward—The Central Office

Monthly status reports
Project progress reports
Work items behind schedule
School problems or concerns
Possible staffing changes
Communication with the Superintendent
Vacation plans
School and staff successes

Laterally—Your Peers

Procedural changes within your school
School innovations
School problems and concerns
School and staff successes

Downward—Your Staff

District policy changes
Upcoming projects
Organizational events
Development opportunities
Changes in school vision, mission, or strategies
Changes in duties and responsibilities

Outward—Your Parents and the General Community

School events
School and student achievement
Change in school policy
School problems and concerns
School projects and programs
Staff achievement

Please modify this checklist to meet your individual situation, adding any communication needs specific to your school.

strongly that school/community relations goes beyond "simply telling the good side of a school's story. Rather, it involves the community in a process of two-way communication with the school." Emphasis focuses on "increasing understanding between the school and its community, not increasing the community's understanding of the school. The aim of public relations programs is to create favorable impressions of the school and community support for the school" (which is a first step). However, fostering open communication within the school-community relations program is "to find ways to involve the community in the educational process" (p. 2).

Do you have an effective school/community relations plan? Pawlas defines this as "a planned, systematic, two-way process of communication between the school and its community to build morale, goodwill, cooperation, and support." If you have not addressed this issue, please consider doing so. You, as the principal, set the pace for what happens or doesn't happen in your school. It is important for you to determine the type, frequency and quality of communications among all members of your school community.

COLLABORATING ON SCHOOL WRITING PROJECTS

Another way you can foster open communication among and between staff, students, and parents is to collaborate on specific written products. As the school principal you probably have already served on many district-level curriculum or policy developing projects; usually a complex report such as a policy manual or a school improvement report is written by the project committee.

We know these tasks can be time consuming. They become even more difficult if we don't like to write. However, these written products are necessary in communicating the school's purpose and even more important in keeping the information channels open. More specifically, these tasks encourage group members to share information and to interact openly and directly on school related issues.

How can you as the school leader facilitate this process? Audrey Joyce (1991) in her book, *Written Communication for School Administrators,* suggests that you organize the work of the writing committee along the four stages of the writing process. These four stages include prewriting, drafting, revising, and editing. Figure 1.2 outlines this process.

FIGURE 1.2. WRITING COMPLEX DOCUMENTS

Prewriting Stage

1. Committee members generate ideas.
2. Committee members seek additional information on assigned topics.
3. Individual committee members report findings of information searches.

Drafting Stage

4. Committee members develop first draft by assigning individuals to write specific sections of the report.

Revising Stage

5. Committee members review first draft, suggest revisions, and rewrite the initial document.

Editing Stage

6. Committee assigns one or more members to review the final draft for content and technical accuracy.
7. Committee reads the final document and approves the report.

According to Joyce (1991), the initial committee meetings are idea-generating sessions with group members discussing what should be included in the document and how it should be organized. During the prewriting stage (Step 1) effective brainstorming strategies such as mindmapping and free writing allow all members of the committee to participate in the process.

This phase may take several sessions until the committee has clearly established the purpose of the document, the intended audience, and the organizational framework. When this has been determined, then individual committee members may be assigned to research parts of the report or to seek additional information (Step 2). These individuals then report back (Step 3) to the committee their findings. The committee then discusses the findings of the research team and uses this information to make any modifications to the organizational framework of the document.

When this stage is completed, the committee moves into the drafting phase. Now individual committee members must work independently (Step 4) to write the various sections of the document. When completed, the first drafts are brought back to the committee (Step 5) for review and discussion. The purpose of this feedback session is to generate revisions for the writers to incorporate in the next draft. This revision process may go through several more meetings until the entire committee approves the final version.

After the drafting and revision stages are completed, one member (Step 6) of the committee may be asked to prepare the final document for printing. This responsibility includes editing the document to make sure there are no technical errors. When the final copy is produced, several committee members (Step 7) may review the document before it is printed and distributed. "The final document then represents the work of the entire committee rather than the work of one individual" (Joyce, 1991, p. 17).

What types of school writing projects could you develop using this process as a guide for the writing team?

Review the four stages of the writing process and decide who on your staff could be resource experts to serve as team members or writing coaches.

Exercise 1.4
DEVELOPING A SCHOOL/COMMUNITY PUBLIC RELATIONS PLAN

Directions: Using Joyce's process for developing a complex document, write a school/community public relations plan. Use the information in your communication inventory to guide your scheme. To assist you in developing this plan Pawlas (1995) provides ten objectives for you to consider:

1. Obtain accurate information about your school.
2. Provide current data about the community.
3. Assert school's credibility.
4. Secure community support.
5. Establish common goals through school improvement teams.
6. Focus on the importance of education for community success.

7. Keep the community informed of important trends.
8. Foster a continuous exchange of information through team building.
9. Assess the school's program through informal and formal channels.
10. Advertise successful achievement to promote community pride toward the school. (pp. 12-14)

PRINCIPALS ON-LINE

What better way to collaborate on writing projects than by getting peer assistance? The internet connection through your computer system may be your best source of help. If you have a specific question or school-related problem then ask around.

However, instead of just referring to colleagues in your own school system, you have the option of starting with the Internet Connection message board. Through computer technology you can post questions and receive replies from other principals and educators who have experienced a similar situation. For example, let's say you have a writing assignment that is difficult for you. It's just tough getting started. You can turn to your computer and through such programs like America OnLine, Prodigy, and the World Wide Web, you can post your question, dilemma, or situation and receive replies from other principals or educators who have dealt with a similar writing problem. In a few minutes or by the end of the day, your colleagues throughout the nation will have faxed you multiple suggestions and even sample responses for your perusal.

Here's just a sample of what is available to you on the information highway:

- **THE NEWSSTAND,** contains educational news items hot off the wires, feature articles from prestigious magazines, and a searchable data base of information about more than 300 magazines.
- **THE RESOURCE PAVILION,** where experts and educational organizations with particular expertise wait to answer educators' questions.
- **THE IDEA EXCHANGE,** a message board center used for the creative exchange of information and ideas on a variety of topics.

- **NASSP ON LINE,** where principals can tap into the database that focuses on the information and issues important to school leaders. E-Mail: nassp @nassp.org.

SUMMARY AND TIPS

Direct and open communication with others develops trust, strengthens the flow of information, and builds better working relationships in your school community. Considering the fact that the general public does not have enthusiastic confidence in the nation's public schools (Elam et al., 1993), principals must make sure that their public knows that they are doing a good job. This requires solid two-way communication skills and techniques (Pawlas, 1995). Specifically, principals need to understand the importance of identifying both the internal and external public and then determine ways to increase communication and feedback.

Consider the following tips to increase such communication in your learning community:

- Encourage your staff to keep one another informed.
- In staff meetings work on two-way communication by seeking agenda items from staff members and allowing them time to raise issues of concern.
- Identify the key people in your school community and make a special effort to keep them informed.
- Don't gloss over anything that creates problems. Report the situation accurately and in a timely manner.
- Seek out communication breakdowns among and between staff members, parents, students, and peers. Devise ways to correct them.
- Double check all written communication before mailing: also ask yourself, "Who could benefit from this information?"
- At the end of the school day ask yourself what happened that should be reported to other individuals.
- Respond to notes, letters, and other requests so individuals know what you are doing about their concerns.
- Establish a systematic school-community public relations program.

RESOURCES

BOOKS AND ARTICLES

Title: *Principle-Centered Leadership*
Author: Stephen R.Covey
Publisher: Summit Books, 1991

The author asserts that leaders and organizations cannot be content with the status quo. Topics for discussion include six conditions for effectiveness, how to understand people's potential rather than just their behavior, and patterns of organizational excellence.

Title: *The Leadership Challenge*
Author: James Kouzes and Barry Posner
Publisher: Jossey-Bass, 1987

The authors show that leadership is a process that involves basic practices and specific skills—all of which can be learned and used by leaders at all levels.

Title: *If It Ain't Broke...BREAK IT*
Author: Robert J. Kriegel and Louis Patler
Publisher: Warner Books, 1991

The authors present ways to increase productivity and quality in various organizations through the use of tools that encourage risk-taking.

Title: *The Official America Online for Windows Tour Guide*
Author: Tom Lichty
Publisher: Ventana Press, 1994

The author shows you how to make the most of your computer. He presents everything you need to know about a national online service such as: building your software library, communicating via e-mail across the nation, sharing common interests and skills, and keeping current with the latest news and information.

SEMINARS AND WORKSHOPS

The workshops and seminars listed in this guide were chosen for their appeal to school administrators. Since the publication of this text, some seminars may have been upgraded or replaced and others may no longer be offered. Likewise, costs and locations may have also changed. We recommend that you contact the consulting group directly for current information and availability.

Title: *Writing, Speaking, and Listening for Successful Communication*
Consulting Group: American Management Association
Contact Number: Tel: 518-891-0065

A communication seminar for managers dealing with situation and audience analysis, determining proper communication channels, and writing concise, understandable messages.

Title: *Managing Relationships at Work*
Consulting Group: The Atlanta Consulting Group
Contact Number: Tel: 800-852-8224

This management seminar focuses on creating a more collaborative, open and trusting work environment. Participants examine their own communication styles, learn to manage their credibility, and develop open lines of communication.

Title: *From the Desk of... A Written Communication Program for School Administrators*
Consulting Group: National Association of Secondary School Principals
Contact Number: Tel: 703-860-0200

A developmental program that engages participants in multiple writing tasks based on the job demands in the principalship. Instructional techniques foster building open communication techniques within school settings.

CHAPTER REFERENCES

Aldrich, P. (1882). Adult writers: Some factors that interfere with effective writing. *Research in the Teaching of English,* 16, 298-300.

Conrad, C. (1985). *Strategic organizational communication.* New York: Holt, Rinehart and Winston.

Drake, T., and Roe, W. (1994). *The principalship.* New York: Macmillan College Publishing Company.

Elam, S., Rose, L., and Gallup, A. (1993). *The 25th annual Gallup/Phi Delta Kappa poll of the public's attitudes toward the public schools.* Princeton, NJ: Gallup Organization.

Jackson, T. (1990). *The perfect resume.* New York: Doubleday.

Joyce, A. (1991). *Written communication and the school administrator*. Boston, MA: Allyn and Bacon.

Lichty, T. (1994). *The official America Online for Windows tour guide*. Chapel Hill, NC: Ventana Press.

Pankake, A., Stewart, G.K., & Winn, W. (1990, November). Choices for effective communication: Which channels to use. *NASSP Bulletin*, 53-57.

Pawlas, G. (1995). *The administrator's guide to school-community relations*. Princeton, NJ: Eye On Education.

2

Checking Your Communication Competence

"Every job is a self-portrait of the person who did it. Autograph your work with excellence."
—NASSP Great Quotations

As a school administrator you have developed a large variety of personal and technical tools for dealing with the world around you. You have successfully designed thousands of routines and procedures for handling the day-to-day problems of life from your private life to your professional life. These are your skills, abilities, and personal characteristics. You wouldn't have made it this far if you didn't have them.

And, in the midst of all this, you have developed your own personal agenda of things that turn you on or turn you off: situations that challenge you, sensations that amuse you, types of relationships that nurture you (or scare you), environments in which you feel comfortable or to avoid, activities that contribute to your well-being.

School leaders, in our opinion, who have current information about productive work cultures are far more likely to develop their school's capacity to improve achievement. Similarly, a school leader who has current knowledge about his or her work skills is far more likely to develop a systematic plan to improve his or her personal performance.

In this chapter you will determine your own areas of strength as they pertain to competence in the field of written expression. You will also assess your school's communication effectiveness.

We hope the result of your analysis will enable you to set specific learning goals as you engage in the writing exercises interspersed throughout the text. As you set these learning goals, consider your perception needs and your skill needs; both are necessary for professional development.

FACING YOUR WRITING APPREHENSION

Despite the emphasis placed on the importance of the written communication role, many well-educated professionals are ineffective writers. Even effective school administrators find writing a difficult task. Yet, the skill is essential for both personal and professional success.

Conrad (1985) asserts that people who have developed a wide repertoire of written and oral communication skills and who have learned when and how to use those skills, tend to advance in their careers more rapidly and contribute more fully to the organization than people who have not done so.

School principals must face daily the demand for some form of writing: letters, memos, bulletins, notices, announcements, guides, speeches, and handbooks. Because of this demand, barriers that reduce writing competence should be examined. One such barrier is writing apprehension.

According to Daly (1985), many people are hesitant about and fearful of writing. This apprehension is often reflected in their writing performance. He emphasizes that the way in which individuals write, and even whether or not they engage in writing at all, depends on more than just skill or writing proficiency. The individual must want to write or at the very least find some value in writing. Daly concludes that one's attitude toward writing is just as important to good writing as one's actual writing ability.

Exercise 2.1
WRITING ATTITUDE SURVEY

Let's examine your attitude about writing. On page 25 are a series of statements about writing. There are no right or wrong answers to these statements. Indicate the degree to which each statement applies to you by circling whether you *(1) Strongly Agree (2) Agree (3) Are Uncertain (4) Disagree* or *(5) Strongly Disagree*. Take your time and try to be as honest as possible.

		SA 1	A 2	U 3	D 4	SD 5	SC Scor
*1	I avoid writing whenever possible. *	1	2	3	4	5	
2	'I have no fear of my writing being evaluated.	1	2	3	4	5	
3	I look forward to writing down my ideas.	1	2	3	4	5	
*4	I am afraid of writing when I know it might be evaluated.*	1	2	3	4	5	
*5	My mind seems to go blank when I start writing.*	1	2	3	4	5	
*6	Expressing ideas through writing seems to be wasting time.*	1	2	3	4	5	
7	I would enjoy submitting my writing to magazines for evaluation and publication.	1	2	3	4	5	
8	I like to write my ideas down.	1	2	3	4	5	
9	I feel confident in my ability to express clearly my ideas in writing.	1	2	3	4	5	
10	I like to have my friends read what I have written.	1	2	3	4	5	
*11	I'm nervous about writing *	1	2	3	4	5	
12	People seem to enjoy what I write.	1	2	3	4	5	
13	I enjoy writing.	1	2	3	4	5	
*14	I never seem to be able to write down my ideas clearly.*	1	2	3	4	5	
15	Writing is a lot of fun.	1	2	3	4	5	
16	I like seeing my thoughts on paper.	1	2	3	4	5	
17	Discussing my writing with others is an enjoyable experience.	1	2	3	4	5	
18	It is easy for me to write good letters.	1	2	3	4	5	
*19	I don't think I write as well as most people.*	1	2	3	4	5	
*20	I'm no good at writing.*	1	2	3	4	5	
	TOTAL						

Adapted from the Daly-Miller Writing Apprehension Scale in *When a Writer Can't Write,* Edited by Mike Rose, The Guilford Press, New York, 1985, page 46. Reprinted with permission.

Directions for Scoring Exercise 2.1: Enter the number you circled in the SC column for each statement. *In scoring the items marked with the asterisk, you need to reverse the score.* For example, if you circled 5 in responding to number #20, then you would mark a 1 in the SC column. Items scored a 3, stay the same. Once you have scored each of the items, total your score and place it in the box at the bottom of the SC column. The lowest score you can get is 20 and the highest score is 100.

Your response to the survey indicates your level of writing apprehension. A score of 20 shows very low writing apprehension; a score of 100 shows very high writing apprehension. Where do you fall on the continuum? Mark your score.

LOW 20_______ MODERATE 40-60_______ HIGH 100 _______

A study of 100 principals who took this survey (Podsen, 1987) revealed the following trends:

FIGURE 2.1. WRITING APPREHENSION TRENDS

Apprehension Level	Male Principals	Female Principals
High (70 -100)	25%	7%
Moderately High (43-69)	28%	39%
Moderately Low (31-42)	35%	34%
Low (20-30)	11%	20%

POINTS TO CONSIDER

A key finding of the study shows a significant relationship between writing apprehension levels and principals' performance of job writing tasks.

- Principals with higher levels of writing apprehension performed fewer writing tasks on the job than principals with lower levels of writing anxiety.
- Principals with higher levels of writing apprehension made more technical writing errors.
- Principals with lower writing anxiety communicated in writing more often on a daily, weekly, monthly and quarterly basis.
- Principals with higher levels of writing anxiety com-

municated more often to peers and least often to the central office.

- Principals with low writing apprehension in both genders delegated more writing tasks than principals with high writing apprehension. Male principals at each level of writing apprehension delegated more writing tasks than their female colleagues.

McCroskey (1982) reports that lower levels of communication apprehension are usually associated with higher levels of communication competence. It may benefit you and your school community to determine the levels of writing apprehension of both teachers and students. Research in the area of writing apprehension (Daly, 1985) indicates the following patterns:

- Individuals with positive attitudes about writing show higher levels of confidence and improvement in their writing.
- Teachers with high writing anxiety assign fewer writing tasks to students than teachers with low writing anxiety.
- Language Arts teachers demonstrate lower writing apprehension levels than math and science teachers.
- Individuals with high writing anxiety not only write fewer documents but produce written messages significantly shorter and less fluent.

We hope you will consider the importance of your writing attitude on your job performance. As the instructional leader in your school, this awareness may assist you in helping yourself and others in communicating more effectively.

SELF-ASSESSMENT PROFILE

Your attitude about writing sets the stage for many of the tasks facing you as a school administrator. Our experience with hundred of principals who have participated in NASSP's writing program *From the Desk Of...* discloses that while most principals are anxious about their writing and fear evaluation of their documents, the feedback they receive during the workshop improves their attitude by providing specific information on their writing strengths (and there are many) as well as areas for growth.

Exercise 2.2
WRITING BEHAVIOR INVENTORY

Let's continue our self-assessment process by focusing on our writing behaviors. Please respond to each item accurately and honestly using one of the following responses: *Always Do (AD), Generally Do (GD), Sometimes Do (SD), Never Do (ND).*

WRITING BEHAVIORS	AD	GD	SD	ND
I set aside a specific time during the day to work on writing tasks.				
I gather information I need before I begin writing.				
I use prewriting techniques to generate ideas. (EX. outlining, mindmapping, freewriting)				
I identify the specific purpose for each document.				
I usually develop a working draft.				
I review my draft for style, purpose, and audience.				
I develop a second draft.				
I proofread to check for common writing errors.				
I am sensitive to my audience's problem or concern.				
I avoid educational jargon.				
My writing presents a professional image.				
I have developed routines to organize incoming paperwork and answer routine correspondence.				
I use a computer to produce my written materials.				
I submit all written reports on time.				
I collaborate with staff on documents.				
I often seek feedback on my documents.				
TOTAL				

These items correspond to the writing behaviors of very effective writers. Analyze your writing patterns. Any areas you have marked ***never do*** and ***sometimes do*** may be areas that need to be investigated. For further explorations of these topics we recommend reading Audrey Joyce's book entitled, *Written Communication and the School Administrator.* The author provides detailed content and specific examples to assist you in expanding your knowledge and skill in performing these behaviors.

Exercise 2.3
COMMON ERRORS WRITING TEST

The following diagnostic test may help you identify what common errors you may need to review. According to Joyce (1991) there are twelve areas that "plague even experienced writers." Answers and explanations follow the diagnostic test. (Joyce, A. Copyright (c) 1991 by Allyn and Bacon. Reprinted with permission)

Directions: Identify the error in each sentence below. Choose the letter A through D of the underlined section that contains the error.

1. After the spring vacation, the school district will hold a series of
A B
evening workshops for it 's administrators with parents and other
C D
interested members of the community.

2. Additional computers were purchased as funds became available, and
A B
the media specialist also bought two new encyclopedias.
C D

3. After debating the issues for three months, the state board approved an
A B
alternate certification plan for teachers, which upset many educators.
C D

4. The State Department of Education is commited to permitting teachers,
A
regardless of their age, to retire after 25 years of service.
B C D

5. Every teacher who wants to individualize instruction must make sure that
A B
all their teacher-made materials meet instructional objectives and state
C D
requirements.

6. A satellite-delivered news program has been piloted in this district before
A B
lunch and found to be very successful in interesting students in the news.
C D

7. Serving as a liason between the task force and the media, the principal
A B
clearly demonstrated his outstanding skills in interpersonal relationships.
C D

8. Everyone who takes advanced placement classes are required to pass the
A B
examination with a score of 3 or better to receive college credit.
C D

9. The success of the athletic departments fund raising has made the
A
student council reassess its fund-raising activities and bookkeeping
B C D

10. The national group of parents went to Washington and charges that the
A B
testing program is sexually biased.
C D

ANSWERS AND EXPLANATIONS TO DIAGNOSTIC TEST

1. Answer C	The possessive form *its* should be used.
2. Answer D	Shift from passive verb in the first section of the sentence to an active verb in the second part.
3. Answer D	There is no clear antecedent for *which.*
4. Answer A	*Committed* is the correct spelling.
5. Answer C	The pronoun *his* should be used instead of *their.*
6. Answer C	The modifier *before lunch* needs to be placed after *program.*
7. Answer A	The word is spelled *liaison.*
8. Answer B	The verb *are* does not agree with the subject *everyone.*
9. Answer A	An apostrophe is needed in *department's.*
10. Answer B	Shift in tense from past to present.

Joyce, A.(1991). *Written Communications and the School Administrator.* Allyn and Bacon: Boston. This diagnostic test is taken from pages 223-225 and 233. Reprinted with permission.

How many did you find? Which ones did you miss? You might want to edit your upcoming writing products for these consistently troublesome areas. William Safire (1979) has developed the largest collection of FUMBLERULES of grammar. Here's our rendition of his "never-say-neverisms."

- Avoid run-on sentences they are often found in one-sentence paragraphs.
- "Don't use no double negatives."
- "Verbs has to agree with their subjects."
- "No sentence fragments."
- Check your draft to see if you any words out.
- Avoid commas, that are not necessary, and should be avoided.

- When you reread your writing, you will discover on rereading that a lot of repetition can be eliminated by rereading, editing, and proofing.
- And don't begin your sentences with conjunctions.
- Editing ruthlessly, dangling participles can be avoided.
- All Principles should complete reports on time: beware of words that sound alike
- "Remember to never split an infinitive."
- The passive voice should be avoided by effective writers.
- The absolute worst troublesome area is the hyperbole.
- Avoid clichés like the plague. Remember effective writing is not a twist of fate.

Adapted from William Safire, "The Fumblerules of Grammar," in *Business Communications* by Golen, Figgins, Smeltzer (1984), NY: Wiley & Sons, 65-66.

For more practice and information in identifying and correcting common writing errors, Joyce's book, *Written Communication and the School Administrator,* is an excellent reference guide for school administrators. However, technology has also afforded us the tools to help make our written work technically correct and exceptionally readable.

Now that you have had the opportunity to examine your writing attitude and behaviors, let's shift your focus to the communication practices in your school.

Exercise 2.4
ASSESSING YOUR SCHOOL'S COMMUNICATION EFFECTIVENESS

Directions: School leaders can use this instrument to assess the strengths and weaknesses of their existing communications process and to plan for needed changes. Please answer each question to the best of your ability. Ask staff members to respond. Check the most appropriate column for each question. The rating scale is as follows:

1. Usually or Strongly

2. Sometimes or Satisfactory
3. Rarely or Marginal
4. Never or Deficient
5. Unknown or Not Applicable

Section I–COMMUNICATION ETHICS- relates to proper communications practices.

	1	2	3	4	5
Confidential information is clearly identified and protected.					
Information is provided internally before it is released to public.					
All affected persons are informed of expectations, rights, responsibilities, and precautions..					
Staff is supplied the necessary information to do their jobs well.					

Section II–COMMUNICATION CLIMATE–refers to the general perception your staff has about the school.

	1	2	3	4	5
Staff members feel respected, listened to, understood, and responded to.					
A feeling of mutual trust exists among staff members and between administration and staff.					
Sensitive problems and serious conflicts are faced and discussed candidly.					
The opportunity for input exists before important decisions are made and actions are taken.					

Section III–COMMUNICATIONS CHANNELS–are the routes or levels by which information flows within the school community.

	1	2	3	4	5
Procedures are clear for organizing and coordinating all important messages.					
Information channels are known and understood.					
Certain staff positions or levels of administration are viewed as frequent communication bottlenecks.					
Upward communication (from staff to principal) and downward communication (from principal to staff) is fast and accurate..					
The grapevine is alive and well used.					

Section IV–COMMUNICATION METHODS–include techniques, devices, or media.

	1	2	3	4	5
A variety of communications methods are used to convey information.					
Important information is presented both verbally and in writing.					
A great deal is placed on written communications.					
The communications methods used are effective.					

Section V–WRITTEN METHODS–relates to the scope of your written communication strategies.

	1	2	3	4	5
• Memoranda					
• Informal notes					
• Staff handbook					
• Routine bulletins					
• Suggestion boxes					
• Bulletin boards					
• Reports					
• Newsletters					
• Outside message boards					
• E-Mail					

Section V–MESSAGE CONTENT–is the substance of the written communication.

	1	2	3	4	5
Message content is factual, accurate, and correct.					
Message is clearly organized using a specific organizational strategy.					
The purpose of the message is stated.					
Wording is adapted to meet the needs of the reader.					

Section VI–COMMUNICATIONS TIMING–involves such factors as: (1) frequency, (2) spacing, and (3) circumstances when a message is sent and received.

	1	2	3	4	5
The timing of important information is carefully planned and coordinated to increase effectiveness.					
Necessary information reaches staff, parents, and students when needed.					
Questions and requests are responded to promptly.					
Communications are continuous and organized rather than occasional and spur of the moment.					
Notice about deadlines and important activities is given sufficiently in advance.					
Urgent information reaches staff promptly.					

Section VII–FEEDBACK TO COMMUNICATIONS– involves getting a response from the intended audience that shows the content is understood.

	1	2	3	4	5
A system exists for verifying that important communications are received.					
Procedures are established to verify that the content of important written messages is understood.					
The process of giving and receiving feedback on one's writing is valued and rewarded.					
The principal solicits ideas and suggestions for improving both internal and external communication concerning the school's operation.					

Section VIII–SOURCES OF INFORMATION–include: (1) other people, (2) personal observation, and (3) documentation.

	1	2	3	4	5
All important information is written down and accessible.					
The policy manual is available and contains up-to-date and complete information.					
You have ready access to a computer to gain information.					
A communication program (plan) exists for crisis situations.					

Exercise 2.5
EXAMINING SCHOOL COMMUNICATION TRENDS

Go back now and tally your responses for each descriptor within the eight communication practices. Summarize your strengths and growth targets. Compare your responses to staff responses.

COMMUNICATION PRACTICES	1 Usually	2 Sometimes	3 Rarely	4 Never	5 Not Known
Communication Ethics (4)					
Communication Climate (4)					
Communication Channels (5)					
Communication Methods (4)					
Written Methods (10)					
Message Content (4)					
Communications Timing (6)					
Feedback to Communications (4)					
Sources of Information (4)					
Total Responses (45)					

ASSESSING YOUR TECHNOLOGICAL IQ

Just a few short years ago this section would be about typewriters. But today we are able to access the most significant aid for school professionals—the word processor and specifically, the home/personal computer. The enormous expansion of these tools has put before us the opportunity to produce high-production, high-quality document output from our computers or word processors. If you don't have access to these resources or, if you do and you are not utilizing them to their fullest capabilities, your career is in jeopardy. That's a strong statement but let's consider the facts.

THE INTERNET

The Internet is a worldwide network of computer networks. It is comprised of thousands of separately administered networks of many sizes and types. Each of these networks is comprised of as many as tens of thousands of computers; the total number of individual users of the Internet is in the millions. ARE

YOU ONE IN A MILLION? This high level of connectivity fosters an unparalleled degree of communication, collaboration, resource sharing, and information access.

As educators we are faced with a threefold challenge made more difficult by the volume and complexity of information now available to all citizens:

1. How to access information;
2. How to find the best information for a given task; and
3. How to make sense of the information both for our own personal use and for the betterment of the schools in which we work.

Research trends in technology assessment show that there is a steady decline in publications in paper format and an increase in electronic formats among and between all public and private agencies (Office of Technology Assessment, 1988).

We are in the information business. As school leaders we must be able to navigate skillfully the growing web of interconnected electronic data bases. Our teachers and students must also be able to tap into the vast information systems now available. More important, providing a gateway to the information highway is not enough. As educators we must be able to hone our own information problem-solving skills if we are to keep our knowledge base current and use the information to construct future knowledge.

ELECTRONIC MAIL

People over thirty remember the day when the phrase "the mail" meant only one thing—envelopes, letters, postmen, mailboxes, and the post office. In those days there was no UPS, no fax, no FEDEX, no e-mail, and no Internet.

The information age is here. It requires another way of communicating, including overnight package delivery, facsimile, voice mail, and e-mail. Each offers a unique service. Electronic mail offers immediacy, convenience, multiple addressing, and automated record keeping.

As a principal, an e-mail system in your home, office, school, and school district can save you time and money. "Nothing matches the convenience, immediacy and ecology of electronic mail" (Lichty, 1994, p. 73). Composing a message amounts to typing it, mailing it with a single click of the mouse to one person or fifty, and filing it on the host computer.

Can you picture the day when all classrooms will have computers at each desk and you can communicate with staff and students without using the intercom, the **PLEASE READ** memos, and a myriad of forms? Your computer e-mail system will obediently hold your mail until you're ready to read it, announce its availability, and never send you junk mail. Are you utilizing this service through your home or office? If not, why not?

WORD PROCESSING, LAYOUT, AND PRODUCTION

Before that written document of yours is seriously read by a staff member, colleague, or parent, it has to pass what we call the *grabber test*—that three- to four-second glance in which the reader decides whether or not it's worth reading now or ever. How many times have you scanned a newspaper or a magazine to decide which articles or advertisements are worth reading?

In today's workplace, skills may not be enough—packaging counts. The underlying assumption is this: If you can't communicate about yourself and your school in a way that invites interest and attention, you aren't *perceived* fully capable to deal with today's highly communications-oriented work world. Like it or not, that's the way it is.

By knowing the basics and developing your ability to tap into the power of your word processing software, you can accomplish the following:

1. Store a large number of sample letters, memos, reports, newsletters, forms, agenda, etc., related to the operation of your school. This will allow you to put together a variety of versions or formats for future use and to strategically determine which approach is best for any given situation.
2. Edit your written work easily and quickly. Most software packages offer editing tools such as spell check, grammar check, thesaurus, and word count for readability indicators.
3. Offer graphic design options which allow you to include graphs, tables, charts, pictures, and clip art.
4. Provide a wide variety of formatting options through font styles and size, borders and shading, and style templates for brochures, fax cover sheets, letters, memos, press releases, presentations, reports, résumés, and manuals.

5. Move text easily within a document or between documents concurrently.
6. Work with long reports by helping you to outline and organize your document, create tables of contents and indexes, and customize footnotes and endnotes.

SUMMARY AND TIPS

The purpose of this chapter is to help you focus on your communication competence in the following areas:

- Your attitude toward writing
- Your daily writing behaviors
- Your knowledge of common writing errors
- Your perception of your school's communication effectiveness
- Your technological withitness

Exercise 2.6
MY COMMUNICATION PROFILE

Directions: Write what you have learned about yourself in each of these areas. What further information do you need? What have you learned about your school?

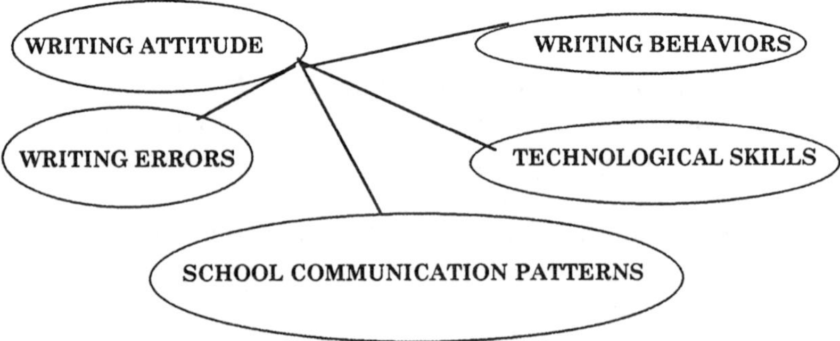

RESOURCES

BOOKS AND ARTICLES

Title: *If You Can Talk, You Can Write*
Author: Joel Salzman
Publisher: Warner Books, 1993

The author provides a humorous approach in dealing with such topics as writer's block and writing anxiety. Practical tips and strategies for getting started and producing effective writing are highlighted.

Title: *Essential Software for Writers*
Author: Hy Bender
Publisher: Writer's Digest, 1994

Details about dozens of programs, from word processors to idea generators to research tools to desk top publishing software; what they do, how to get them, how they benefit you and your writing.

SEMINARS AND WORKSHOPS

The workshops and seminars listed in this guide were chosen for their appeal to school administrators. Since the publication of this text, some seminars may have been upgraded or replaced and others may no longer be offered. Similarly, costs and locations may have changed. We recommend that you contact the consulting group directly for current information and availability.

Title: *Management of Technology for School Administrators*
Consulting Group: National Association of Secondary School Principals
Contact Number: Tel: 800-253-7746 Ext. 330

In partnership with The Astronauts Memorial Foundation's Educational Technology Institute, NASSP offers a seminar to train school leaders for implementing and using technology in their schools.

CHAPTER REFERENCES

Conrad, C. (1985). *Strategic organizational communication*. New York: Holt, Rinehart and Winston.

Daly, J. (1985). Writing apprehension. In M.Rose (Ed.), *When a writer can't write* (pp. 43-82). New York: The Guilford Press.

Joyce (1991). *Written communication and the school administrator.* Boston, MA: Allyn and Bacon.

Lichty, T. (1994). *The official America Online for Windows tour guide.* Chapel Hill, NC: Ventana Press.

McCroskey, J.C. (1982). Communication competence and performance. *Communication Education*, 31, 1-8.

Podsen I. (1987). *School administrators: The role of writing apprehension on job related writing tasks and writing performance.* Unpublished Dissertation. Atlanta, GA: Georgia State University.

Office of Technology Assessment (1988). *Informing the nation: Federal information dissemination in an electronic age.* Report No. OTA CTT 397. Washington, DC.

St. John, W. (1990, December). Assessing the communications effectiveness of your school. *NASSP Practitioner,* VOL XVII, No. 2.

Tennant, R., Ober, J., and Lipow, A. (1993). *Crossing the internet threshold: An instructional handbook.* Berkeley, CA: Library Solutions Press.

PART TWO

DISPLAYING AUDIENCE SAVVY

"As soon as you move one step up from the bottom, your effectiveness depends on your ability to reach others through the written word."

—Peter Drucker

WHAT YOU NEED TO KNOW

Both oral and written communication skills are important in any leadership role. However, research findings show a growing trend for written communication proficiency to affect job promotion and supervisory effectiveness. A recurring problem in written communication for adult writers centers on the following issue: *Planning of the writing product, including making preliminary decisions about purpose, organization, and audience.*

Aldrich (1982) surveyed 165 top and mid-level business managers working in various fields who had moved into management positions and found writing to be a component of the job.

These professionals indicated that promotion depended on their ability to write well; ineffective writing slowed down or prevented them from moving to top executive positions. The researcher concluded that the majority of these adult writers did not know that they needed to make preparatory decisions about the purpose, points, and audience of their written documents (Day, 1981).

Although most of the managers demonstrated grammatical and mechanical proficiency, the majority were considered to be ineffective writers within their organization. Demographic data showed that more than half did not have training in writing beyond freshman composition; the others had taken college courses or writing workshops offered by employers.

Eight areas that emerge as problem areas for adult writers in business leadership positions are:

- *Conciseness*
- *Clarity of meaning*
- *Success in communicating the purpose*
- *Spelling*
- *Sentence clarity and variation*
- *Paragraph organization*
- *Document organization*

Likewise, for adult writers in educational leadership, one researcher found that administrators showed problems in spelling, lengthy paragraphs containing several ideas, incorrect use of pronouns, and punctuation errors (Humble, 1985). In addition, Humble concluded that the participants in her study demonstrated a weakness in their ability to respond in clear, simple terms. She reported, "The interns had considerable difficulty changing their vocabulary for different audiences" (p. 61). Humble concluded that leadership preparation programs should include a course in "school-community relations with emphasis on how to communicate more effectively and more cordially with parents."

According to Wycoff (1991), "writing abilities are as visible as a person's wardrobe. Impressions may last even longer, as files containing written work are read and reread." You may be bright and hardworking, but poor writing skills "will stall your career climb on the lower rungs of the ladder" (p. 64).

KNOWING YOUR AUDIENCE

The chapters in this section deal with audience. Based on what we know about the principalship and what school administrators have told us in many writing workshops, we have presented this topic by contact frequency. Principals communicate in writing most often to staff, then to parents, followed by the central office. After attending to these audiences, principals write to peers, and finally to the general community (Podsen, 1987).

Each chapter examines the special characteristics of a particular audience. The goal is for you to learn more about each audience so your writing will be focused and tailored to its needs and perceptions. The result will be a clearer document because you have strategically planned the outcome of your message.

Exercise
PRINCIPALS' WRITING INVENTORY

Directions: Below are statements about writing. The purpose of the inventory is to help you determine the variety of writing activities and audiences you engage in on the job. There are no right or wrong answers. Check only one response. A *NO* response shows an activity you are not doing now. A *DELEGATED* response indicates a writing task you do but have assigned to someone else. A *YES* response shows an activity you are doing now. For both *Delegated* and *Yes* responses please circle how often you do this writing task: D-daily, W-weekly, M-monthly, Q-quarterly, and Y-yearly. Take your time and try to be as accurate as possible.

STAFF	NO	YES	DEL	DWM	QY
1. I write a staff newsletter.					
2. I develop teacher handbooks.					
3. I have a substitute teacher guide.					
4. I develop staff surveys.					
5. I write summaries of school board meetings.					
6. I prepare written agendas before staff meetings.					
7. I respond in writing to staff concerns.					
8. I write thank you notes.					
9. I send special occasion cards and notes.					
10. I generate school calendars.					
11. I reinforce verbal requests.					

12. I write letters of recommendation.					
13. I document teacher/staff behaviors in writing.					
14. I write descriptive narratives of teacher performance.					
15. I script classroom observations.					
16. I write letters of staff commendation.					
TOTAL YOUR YES/ NO/ DEL/ RESPONSES					

PARENTS	NO	YES	DEL	DWM	QY
1. I write welcome letters to new parents.					
2. I write a school newsletter.					
3. I produce brochures, packets, or pamphlets to highlight school programs, activities, student achievement.					
4. I have a parent handbook.					
5. I generate surveys for parent input or assessment.					
6. I respond in writing to parent concerns or criticisms.					
7. I send thank your notes.					
8. I write to parents recognizing their child's behavior and/or achievement.					
9. I send special purpose bulletins to inform parents of important issues and/or problems.					
10. I have a parent-teacher conference guide.					
11. I create flyers or posters to advertise school events.					
12. I provide parents a school calendar of events.					
13. I write letters of commendation.					
TOTAL YOUR YES/ NO/ DEL/ RESPONSES					

STUDENTS	NO	YES	DEL	DWM	QY
1. I have a student handbook.					
2. I publish a student newsletter.					
3. I write welcome letters to new students.					
4. I develop student surveys.					
5. I respond in writing to student questions or concerns.					
6. I send thank you notes to students.					
7. I send special occasion cards or notes.					
8. I produce recognition awards/ certificates.					
TOTAL YOUR YES/ NO/ DEL/ RESPONSES					

PEERS	NO	YES	DEL	DWM	QY
1. I use E-mail.					
2. I keep colleagues informed of school issues, achievements, and events.					
3. I send special occasion notes or cards.					
4. I submit proposals for participation in professional meetings, conferences, and programs.					
5. I recognize the achievements of peers in writing.					
6. I write articles for professional journals.					
TOTAL YOUR YES/NO/DEL/ RESPONSES					

CENTRAL OFFICE	NO	YES	DEL	DWM	QY
1. I write school improvement reports.					
2. I develop professional development plans .					
3. I have a school-community public relations plan.					
4. I complete required paperwork on time.					
5. I keep the superintendent informed.					
6. I use E-mail.					
7. I develop inservice workshops.					
8. I write grants.					
9. I produce annual reports.					
TOTAL YOUR YES/ NO/ DEL/ RESPONSES					

GENERAL COMMUNITY	NO	YES	DEL	DWM	QY
1. I write news releases.					
2. I write news articles about school events/staff/students.					
3. I design questionnaires to survey the local community about the school.					
4. I develop publicity brochures to highlight school programs and achievements.					
5. I respond in writing to questions, concerns, and rumors.					
6. I know the key opinion leaders in the community and keep them informed about important issues					
7. I create posters and flyers to advertise school events.					
8. I have an internet web page about my school.					
TOTAL YOUR YES/NO/ DEL/ RESPONSES					

Exercise
ANALYZING YOUR WRITING PATTERNS

What audiences do you write to most frequently? Are you neglecting a particular audience? Examine your communication methods and channels for each audience. Are you utilizing the variety of options available to you? Look at your contact frequency. Assess your timing of important information. Is there any relationship between your writing apprehension and frequency of job writing?

AUDIENCE	NO	YES	DELEGATED
Staff (16)			
Parents (13)			
Students (8)			
Peers (6)			
Central Office (9)			
General Community (8)			
TOTAL (60)			

Writing Apprehension Score
Low (20-42) Moderate (43-69) High (70-100)

Job Writing Frequency
High (41-60) Moderate (20-40) Low (0-20)

3

WRITING TO STAFF

"If you work for an institution, whatever your job whatever your level, be yourself when you write. You will stand out as a real person among robots."
—William Zinsser

Of all the varied audiences to whom you write, you probably spend more time writing to your staff than any of the others. Consider for a second the many kinds of writing you need to do in relation to your staff. At some time or another you probably engage in at least the following kinds of correspondence:

- sending brief notes to staff members to:
  - thank them for performing some task or favor
  - ask them to assist with some needed task
  - remind them of an upcoming commitment
- composing more formal memos and letters to:
  - follow up on observations and conferences
  - respond to requests for recommendations and endorsements
  - document incidents and conferences
- summarizing committee meetings and meeting with individuals
- writing entries for the daily bulletin or newsletter

You can undoubtedly expand on this list by identifying subtasks or variations for each of those listed. The bottom line is that you, as principal, spend a great deal of time writing to members of your faculty, paraprofessional, clerical, and custodial staff.

Not only is your staff your most frequent audience, it can also seem to be one of the most intimidating and overwhelming.

Some staff members may consider themselves to be saviors of the language and peruse every paragraph to seek out examples to prove their point. Others may have more personal reasons for using the administration's writing style, or lack thereof, as confirmation of their agenda. Still others may simply view your writing as a barometer for assessing how the administration, in general, and you, in particular, are doing.

Whatever their reasons, staff members read the principal's letters, memos, evaluations, notes, announcements, and bulletin notices thoughtfully and, sometimes, critically. You should be especially vigilant, therefore, to ensure that all correspondence with members of the staff adheres to the standards of modern written business English as well as to your personal standards. Let's take a look at what some of those standards might comprise.

GETTING STARTED

Before you even think about putting pen to paper or turning on the computer screen, be sure to ask yourself the two most important questions about any piece of correspondence: Who is my audience? and What is my purpose in writing to this audience?

WHO IS MY AUDIENCE?

What do I know about this audience that should influence any aspect of my writing? Have my previous experiences been positive, negative, or neutral? Have I established a history with this audience? Does this audience have any personal needs, interests, experiences, personal situations about which I should be aware and which should influence my approach to the situation?

In other words, it is important to take into consideration everything you already know about your audience and about your relationship to that audience before you begin to address the situation. With many members of the staff, such knowledge and insight may come automatically to you because of your history with that person. For others, you may need to think more consciously and carefully to identify those characteristics which you need to consider. Whatever the case, the important thing is to be certain you have identified your audience and that you have determined what you need to know to address that audience effectively.

WHAT IS MY PURPOSE IN WRITING TO THIS AUDIENCE?

Why am I writing to this audience? When addressing the staff, this question implies two considerations:

- Could my purpose be accomplished in some manner other than through writing? Could I walk down the hall and deliver the message verbally? Would that be a better way of conveying the message? Is it really necessary to write?
- Once I've determined that a written form is the proper mode of communication for this particular message, what do I hope to accomplish through this correspondence? Do I expect the audience to do something as a result? Do I simply want the audience to know something? What are the expectations that have caused me to write?

The failure to ask these vital questions probably lies at the heart of most failed correspondence. When people don't ask these questions, they usually flounder and write aimlessly, often writing around and around the actual subject without ever coming to grips with it because they have not properly identified the subject for themselves.

The positive side of that coin is that when writers do ask these questions, they provide the kind of focus and direction which allows them to write clearly, succinctly, and effectively. They know where they want to go and what they want to accomplish. Having identified these two goals, their writing often flows effortlessly and accomplishes what they expect.

If you are not already in the habit of very consciously identifying your *audience* and *purpose* before you begin writing, you might find it very helpful to start writing the two words right at the top of your memo pad or typing them right at the top of your computer screen before you begin every piece of writing for a while. Make it part of your writing routine. Then make sure you identify both characteristics as clearly possible. You will soon find that doing so will make your writing flow more smoothly.

DO'S AND DON'TS

Once you have established the custom of clearly identifying your audience and purpose for each piece of correspondence, consider the following ideas to tighten up your prose and further guarantee the likelihood of communicating its message clearly and effectively.

Make your writing sound personal. Far too much educational writing sounds as if it came from a machine or a committee. Make your writing sound like it was written by a person, in fact, a very special person—you. Feel free to use the words *I* and *me*. There is nothing wrong with these words if they're used correctly. Somewhere in elementary school many people learned to avoid such words, undoubtedly so that they would not overuse them. While your memos and letters should not be peppered with these two personal pronouns, you need not shun them completely.

It is equally true that personal words such as *you, we,* and *us* add power and familiarity to your writing. Telling a member of the faculty that *"I would really like you to serve on the School Improvement Team"* is far more personal and clear than *"It will be necessary for someone in your department to...."* or *"One must always be ready to assist by serving on faculty committees designed to strengthen the instructional program."*

One pronoun you probably want to avoid is *myself.* While there is nothing wrong with the word, it is currently being misused a great deal by people who are not comfortable using *I* and *me*. The only time you should use the word *myself* is if you have already used *I* earlier in the sentence and you want to say that something happened to you. For example, it is correct to say: *"I cut myself" or "I hurt myself" or "I saw myself becoming superintendent."* However, instead of writing, *"Please see my secretary to arrange a meeting with Ms. Anderson and myself"* you should write:*"Please see my secretary to arrange a meeting with Ms. Anderson and me."*

Keep your memos and letters brief. Principals are very busy people. So are teachers, counselors, department heads, and other members of the professional and non-professional staff. You will do yourself and them a big favor if you keep your memos and letters very short and completely to the point.

Try forcing yourself to get all of your ideas onto one sheet of paper. If you have done a thorough job of identifying your purpose, you should be able to convey your message quickly and concisely. The more you write, the greater will be the opportunities for rambling, for getting lost in your prose, for misleading, and boring your audience, and for being misunderstood. Keep your writing simple. Keep your sentences simple and short. Keep your paragraphs short, probably no longer than four or five sentences. If you are able to keep all of your correspondence short, you will undoubtedly find that you have both clarified your message and delighted your reader.

Avoid repeating yourself. One of the best ways to tighten up your writing so that it is clear and brief is to make sure you do not say the same thing more than once even if you say it in different ways. English is already a highly redundant language. You must ensure that you do not add to the repetition by rephrasing the same ideas and expressing the same thoughts two or three different ways in the same piece of correspondence.

Some people not only repeat ideas but add unnecessary words which are repetitive. For example, in the sentence, "*It is my own personal belief that the magnet school concept can be...*" the word *personal* is not needed. To say something is my belief already communicates the idea that it is a personal one. Similarly, when writing that "*This new language arts program will be evaluated just 12 short months from now,*" the word *short* is not only unnecessary but incorrect. Months are not short or long; they just are.

Be sure to adopt the right tone. If you have taken the time and thought to consider all you know about your intended audience, you need to go the next step by doing all you can to establish the appropriate tone when addressing your topic with that audience. Your first consideration will certainly be to communicate your ideas in a professional tone. You are the principal. You are the chief teacher in your building. You must be sure to teach by example as well as by pronouncement.

The language you use and the tone you establish will tell your audience much about you, about how you perceive the topic, and how you feel about the audience. By keeping your tone entirely detached and level-headed, no matter how frustrated or angry or put upon you might feel, you will have communicated your ability to rise above such considerations to keep the topic on a truly professional level (Johnston, 1994).

If, however, you feel so frustrated or angry or put upon that you feel that you simply must put your ideas into writing, by all means do so. Writing out your anger or frustration will definitely help you clarify exactly what and how you feel about the situation. It is extremely therapeutic to vent yourself on paper or on the screen. So go ahead; write it out. Write it all out. **Just don't send it.** Put it away and don't look at it for at least 24 hours. Then reread it to see whether or not you still feel the same way and whether or not you want that person to know you feel that way. If you still think you want to send it, ask another administrator or a trusted colleague or your mentor or your spouse to read it. Ask that person only to respond to how he or she would feel about receiving the correspondence. Chances are that somewhere along the line you will begin to modify, to soften, to lessen the harshness so that the document will have the proper professional tone for the educational leader of the building to communicate.

Exercise 3.1
TAKING STOCK OF TONE

Pull out copies of staff correspondence over the last few weeks. Try to categorize them by their tone. Pawlas and Meyers (1989) give us a framework to consider in judging our approach.

• Authoritative	This is threatening and cast in iron.
• Collaborative	This respects the expertise of others and encourages shared-decision making.
• Complimentary	This gives someone a pat on the back.
• Supportive	This is constructive criticism with an offer of help
• Informal/Friendly	This acknowledges ongoing professional respect and rapport.
• Objective	This just reports the facts directly and candidly.

Use strong topic sentences. You probably have not had much opportunity to think about topic sentences since Ms. Dove made you do that boring workbook exercise back in the seventh grade. Topic sentences can, however, be very useful tools for both busy writers and busy readers.

First of all, they bring focus to your writing. They force you to come to grips with the essential element of each paragraph. They serve as steps in an outline or a plan. If you begin each paragraph with a strong focusing sentence, you will find that it is easier to write the rest of the paragraph. After you have announced in your topic sentence what the paragraph will be about, you need then only address each step needed to address the topic. If, for example, you open your paragraph by writing, "*The committee will first consider the proposed benefits of adopting a seven-period schedule."* You now know that what you need to complete the paragraph is a list of some of the proposed benefits the committee should consider.

Secondly, strong topic sentences assist busy readers by making it easy for them to scan a piece of correspondence quickly so that they can assess what is being proposed and what is being expected of them. Initially, they do not need to read every word. By running through the topic sentences, they can make well-informed judgments about their involvement in the topic.

Make sure every sentence has a clearly defined subject. Currently, much professional writing in education, and many other fields, is afflicted with the tendency to put almost everything in the passive voice. Such writing obscures who will be responsible for much of the actions discussed. For example, try to determine the persons who are accountable for the following actions:

> *"Teachers will be required to turn in their planning books at the beginning of each week."* (Who is requiring this action?)

> *"Once the parent conference schedule has been agreed upon, teachers will be expected to identify dates where there are conflicts."* (Who is going to agree to the schedule? Who expects the teachers to identify the conflicts?)

These sentences are written in the passive voice. While there is nothing inherently wrong with this form, you should restrict its use. When writers use this style a great deal, their writing becomes weakened because the actual subjects of each sentence are hidden. Take a second look at the above sentences, now written in the active voice. Although you might not like the message, there will be no misunderstanding who will be responsible.

> *"I would like you to turn in your planning books at the beginning of each week."*

> *"Once the committee has decided on the dates for parent conferences, your department chair will ask each of you to identify any dates for which you have conflicts."*

Strive relentlessly to have a clearly defined subject near the beginning of each sentence. If you do so, you will automatically strengthen your writing by eliminating any question of doubtful responsibility. The passive voice lacks authority because it hides the actors. Improve your writing by avoiding it.

Eliminate as much clutter as possible. It is probably impossible to get rid of all of it. Every time you weed out one unnecessary word or expression, another quickly pops up in its place. Our language has become so filled with catch phrases and meaningless words and expressions that it is likely that many of them will creep into our daily speech and writing. It is important, however, to become vigilant about making sure they do not appear in official correspondence. One function of the principal is to set an example for the rest of the staff. That example includes being a model of language excellence. While that does not imply that every memo be a candidate for a Pulitzer prize, it does mean that the principal's correspondence should be free from senseless verbiage.

Not too long ago two high-ranking administrators got together to plan an experiment with language and its effect on their staff. They proposed to create a new word based on a word the staff already knew and to use that word during staff meetings and private conversations. They maintained that within a short period, other administrators would start using it. They settled on the word *succinctly* and began dropping it during staff meetings in sentences like *"Read through this report and see if you can succinctify it for me"* and *"This last paragraph is all right, but it still needs to be succinctified."*

In less than a week at least two other high-level administrators were heard using the term during staff meetings. Within three weeks more than a half-dozen administrators and their secretaries were bandying the term around. The word appeared in at least two memos.

It is very easy for unnecessary and unheard-of words and expressions to cross over into the spoken vocabulary and then into people's writing. A good example is the expression, "at this point in time." It is unlikely that anyone used this expression 25 years ago. They probably said either "now" or "at this point." Because one person used "at this point in time" on national television during a highly provocative hearing, it is now almost impossible for some people to use any other expression. The point is that the expression is redundant; "at this point" already means "now." There is no need for the "in time."

Our language is filled with this kind of unneeded or redundant terms. Such words and phrases clutter up writing. Perhaps more importantly, it convinces our lay public that we are trying to cover up our actions by using language that is indecipherable to the general public.

Avoid jargon, educationese, and pomposity. Another way that educators convince the public that they have a language all their own is the proliferation of the meaningless verbiage which has plagued much of professional writing for years. You can find it in memos, journals, letters to parents, reports to the school board, reports to our political leaders, almost everywhere.

One such example found its way onto the editorial page of a county newspaper under the head: *"We could not've said it better...."*

> *Underlying the efforts of ______ County's Dropout Prevention Plan is the desire to establish and maintain a behavioral and curricular environment in order to promote social bonding among, students, teachers, and members of the larger community, and to be conducive to the educational engagement necessary for learning and developing the requisite skills for a meaningful life. The design and development of the plan presupposes that the diversity among children and young people give way to a multifarious set and differences in degree of wants, needs, desires, and aspirations which oftentimes appear incongruent with the institution's norms and values.*

The quote goes on for two more paragraphs. The editors conclude: *"They call it educationese...and if they don't, they should."* Unfortunately, there are educators (and lawyers, doctors, politicians, and probably postal clerks) who sincerely believe that they should not use a one-syllable word if they can find one with four syllables. They consistently strive to impress through their larger-than-life vocabulary. They usually defeat their own purpose. If clear communication is their goal, as it should be, using big words and convoluted syntax will defeat them every time. The best writing remains the simple writing. Stick to simple words in simple sentences.

Learn to eliminate. Many of the problems that inflict educational writing involve a failure on the part of the writer to go back over the document to eliminate redundancies, inanities, and the other kinds of writing weaknesses already addressed. While it is a good idea when you are writing the first draft to write quickly and smoothly without pausing to correct and edit, it is also extremely important to go back to that draft to weed out the clutter which impedes clear communication. During this phase of the writing process, it is wise to be on the lookout for outdated expressions which get in the way of the personal tone you want to create in your writing.

Expressions like "It seems important to remember that..." and "While it is interesting to note that..." tend to sound as if the principal is purposely attempting to create a gulf between the reader and herself or himself. Reread your manuscript first with the sole purpose of eliminating such lofty and potentially alienating expressions. Keep the language simple and direct.

Proofread, proofread, proofread—then have someone else proofread. After you have reread the first draft to ensure that the language is simple, direct, and clear, go back over it again to make sure that it also is free of technical errors of spelling, punctuation, usage, and capitalization. Nothing will make your writing more susceptible to negative public scrutiny than a misspelled word or a glaring agreement error or the wrong pronoun. Many people who themselves commit the same kinds of mistakes with the mechanics of written English are the first to point out those same errors in others' writing, particularly the boss's. Shield yourself from such reproach by making sure that your writing is technically perfect.

Many administrators feel uncomfortable with the technical side of writing, and they let this concern interfere with their ability to produce clear, flowing sentences and paragraphs. They let themselves be overly conscious of the mechanics while they are writing. Actually, the mechanics are the easiest part of writing. The conventions of capitalization, punctuation, and spelling are not subjective; they are finite and can be mastered far more successfully than can the ability to produce clear, simple, and concise language.

If, however, you do not feel comfortable proofreading your own work, a difficult task for even accomplished writers, enlist the assistance of a valued colleague or another member of the staff. Perhaps you can involve an English teacher or someone with a special proficiency in language arts. You will undoubtedly flatter them by asking to use their special gift to improve the communications between the principal and the staff. Whatever method you choose, make sure that the task gets done. A memo with glaring mechanical errors will quickly make its way around the building.

Exercise 3.2
PEER COACHING

When it comes to writing many educators tend to get long-winded; they often believe there is merit in quantity and quality. Principal Windy composed this memo in draft form before leaving the office. Because you are an effective writer, he has sent you a copy for revisions. Keeping in mind the suggestions outlined in this chapter, rewrite the memo.

TO: G.H. Smith, Superintendent
FROM: R. Windy, Principal
DATE: May 5
SUBJECT: Cooling Inefficiency

Teachers have complained that when the shades are fully lowered they do not effectively sift out the sun's rays especially during the late afternoon hours. This problem is particularly troublesome during the warm months from April through September when the classrooms on the south side of the building really become exceedingly hot.

When the staff brought this problem to my attention some weeks ago, it inaugurated a thorough action research study within the school. Several science teachers decided to use the situation to teach the scientific method to their sixth grade students. Thermometers were placed in all ten classrooms on the south side of the school building and the shades were fully lowered throughout the entire afternoon. Students and teachers recorded readings every hour on the hour. For comparison data, heavy fabric was placed over the windows in two classrooms which were chosen randomly, and the temperature was also recorded hourly during the afternoon hours. During the entire time of the study, all room thermostats were set at 72 degrees with specific instructions not to change the setting for any reason.

At the end of the test period, the following conclusions were made after the data had been gathered, analyzed and compiled. The average temperature in the classrooms with shades was 87 degrees, as recorded by the room thermostats and the test thermometers. However, the temperature in the classrooms with the special cloth covering varied from 72 to 77 degrees as recorded by the room thermostats and the test thermometers. Therefore, the test data indicate that the shades on the south side of the school do not adequately screen out the rays of the son.

Based on this study, a search for curtain material was initiated that would prove effective in filtering out the rays of the sun particularly for classrooms on the south side of the building, The PTA president determined that there are three types of materials currently on the market that would resolve our problem with extreme heat during the months in question. Bids have been requisitioned from several companies who carry these materials. I am requesting financial assistance in procuring these curtains for all classrooms. Particularly, for those classrooms on the south side of the building.

Adapted from Cochran, J. "Filtering the Windy Memo." In *Business Communication* by Golen, Figgins, and Smeltzer (1984). Wiley & Sons, NY, pp. 69-70.

SUMMARY

Principals are incredibly busy people. Probably no one in the school system is already more overburdened than the building administrators. Their tasks are myriad and diverse. They are constantly on center stage. Everything they say, do, and write is observed, reacted to, and scrutinized by their public.

While their actions and statements are always subject to public response and analysis, only their written words will remain for observation after the situation is over. Letters, memos, evaluations, and other written documents become part of a very public record. Principals need to do all they can to guarantee that they have done all they can to prevent their writing from coming back to haunt them at a later time. Principals cannot avoid writing, so they must make sure that their writing will present them in the best possible light. Writing clearly, simply, concisely, and correctly should enable the principal to communicate with authority, humanity, and pride.

RESOURCES

BOOKS AND ARTICLES

Title: *Managing a Diverse Workforce*
Author: John Fernandez
Publisher: Lexington Books, 1991

The author asserts that a leader's ability to get staff of different genders and of different ethnic and cultural backgrounds to work together effectively may be a key factor for organizational success in the future.

SEMINARS AND WORKSHOPS

The workshops and seminars listed in this guide were chosen for their appeal to school administrators. Since the publication of this text, some seminars may have been upgraded or replaced and others may no longer be offered. Similarly, costs and locations may have also changed. We recommend that you contact the consulting group directly for current information and availability.

Title: *From the Desk of... A Written Communication Program for School Administrators*
Consulting Group: National Association of Secondary School Principals
Contact Number: Tel: 703-860-0200

A developmental program that engages participants in multiple writing tasks based on the job demands in the principalship. Instructional techniques foster building open communication techniques within school settings.

Title: *Conflict Analysis and Resolution*
Consulting Group: National Association of Secondary School Principals
Contact Number: Tel: 703-860-0200

A developmental workshop that teaches principals how to assess their current approach to resolving conflict and developing strategies for dealing with conflict situations in schools.

Title: *Managing Differences and Agreements: Making Conflict Work for You*
Consulting Group: Designed Learning, Inc.
Contact Number: Tel: 908-754-5102

This seminar presents effective strategies to help managers deal with people who are angry, emotional, or irrational. Participants develop skills for handling situations where conflict may be caused by time pressures and differences over performance.

CHAPTER REFERENCES

Cochran, J. (1984). Filtering the windy memo. In *Business communication* (pp. 69-70). New York: John Wiley & Sons.

Day, Y. (1981). Wrestling alligators. In S. Golen, R. Figgins, and L. Smeltzer (Ed.), *Business communication* (pp. 50-57). New York: John Wiley & Sons.

Johnston, C. (1994, August). Professional talk. *The Executive Educator*.

Pawlas, G., and Meyers, K. (1989). *The principal and communication*. Bloomington, IN: Elementary Principal Series No. 3. Phi Delta Kappa Educational Foundation.

Wycoff, J. (1991). *Mindmapping*. New York: Berkley Books.

4

Writing to Parents

"Never assume anything about the audience you are writing to; the assumption could prove dangerous."
—Anonymous

Why Is Writing to Parents Tough?

Perhaps the most difficult audience to write to is parents. After all depending upon the size of the school, you may have as few as 500 or as many as 5,000 potential supporters or critics. However, the one thing they all have in common is the need to know how their child is performing in school.

Unlike staff, parents have limited opportunities to meet with us directly and personally. Most often the only interaction the majority of parents have with us is through the written communications we send home. At school our staff has the advantage of knowing us through verbal, written, and interpersonal interactions. We must take the time to do a better job of developing a two-way, collaborative style of communication, if we are to increase our skill in fostering open lines of communication with parents. Most often our writing to parents is direct, formal, and impersonal. Here's one example for you to think about:

Figure 4.1. Parent Letter Expressing Concern Over School Policy and Follow-Up Letter From Principal

Dear Mr. Martin:

Thank you for meeting with my husband and me. Since our meeting I have found my disillusionment with changing school policy has grown to the point that I feel it fails to reflect the basic premise of the educational system and flies in the face of current practice.

Unionville is moving away from assessing children based on their actual abilities. In the name of easy sorting, a standardized test is being elevated to the point of ensuring Aldous Huxley's *Brave New World* will soon envelop our school system. As mentioned in the enclosed article, *Tracked to Fail,* "we are becoming a society where test-taking skills are the prerequisites for a chance at getting a good education, and where hard work, hope, and ambition are in danger of becoming nothing more than meaningless concepts." To that I will add that earning A's in all subject areas, excelling in the classroom and in the Quest Program, and being named on the high honor roll all year in the Unionville School District are also meaningless achievements.

In second grade my daughter was identified and selected for the enrichment program. She has been part of the Quest Program, receiving outstanding reports for her work. I have enclosed her current performance appraisals from Quest. Throughout third and fourth grade my daughter has shown her ability in the classroom earning consistently high grades in all subject areas. She has been cited each quarter on the high honor roll. However, my daughter, Jacqueline, is being excluded from the High Achievers Honors Fifth Grade Class because she missed four questions on the Reading Comprehension portion of the MAT. Apparently, her outstanding scholastic achievement and her proven ability mean nothing nor do the recommendations of her teachers. My daughter and other less able test-takers have proven their academic ability for three years. Yet, despite those consistent achievements, the game is rigged against them when an MAT score eclipses all else.

Moreover, the body of educational literature abounds with information on standardized testing and defensible criteria. Enclosed is an article which states "students participating in programs for the gifted and talented should meet criteria that are defensible given our current knowledge of human potential. Any single measure is unlikely to be sufficient justification for including or excluding a child." This seems to be the crux of the problem for poor test-takers. Most programs use a combination of criteria in the selection process.

It is my belief that using one test criterion for honors ability/eligibility discriminates against those high achieving honor students who are poor test-takers. Is ease of sorting the new goal of the district? If it is then a faulty and myopic vision will lead our school district into the next century. Past criteria for selection for enrichment/honors programs have been multifaceted, including MAT test results, the Torrence test, grade level performance and teacher recommendation. Why was this process changed especially when it reflected best practice described in the current education journals?

I, therefore, request that you enlarge the class so that these students who have proven their ability are not robbed of a unique irreplaceable opportunity which they have earned. What message is sent to such a student? Is a one day a year test score more important than three years' worth of accomplishments? I also urge you to reevaluate the present selection process for the school's gifted and talented program based on the current literature. The enclosed articles address these issues.

Thank you for your thoughtful consideration.

Sincerely,

Barbara Clough

Dear Mrs. Clough:

I am writing in response to our meeting as well as your letter of July 19, 199_, which you also sent to the Board of Education. Nearly a year ago, after reviewing the procedures for admission to the Quest Program, I determined that several students should be "Grandfathered" into the program for an additional year based on the fact that MAT's had not been administered for a couple of years even though they are supposed to be used as criteria for the program.

At that time, I wrote to you and informed you that in order for students to be in the program or in a high achieving class they must score at a certain level on the MAT's. The use of standardized test results as the main criteria for admission into these types of programs is used in almost every district that has such programs. For the 1995-96 school year, some students who scored particularly high in reading but not over the 75th percentile in math were granted admittance in order for us to have a large enough class to operate the program. Math and reading percentiles were not averaged because the emphasis of the program is on reading/language arts.

I am sure that your daughter, as others who performed well in their classes and were not eligible, will continue to do well in her studies. While I know that you are disappointed in the process and philosophically do not agree with it, nonetheless it is our procedure. In other districts, with which I am familiar, the criteria are even more rigid.

As a parent, you obviously spend a great deal of time nurturing Jacqueline's thirst for learning. As you know, she has been placed with a team of enthusiastic and skilled teachers who should be able to meet her needs and continue to help her grow academically.

Sincerely,

Edward Martin
Principal

Exercise 4.1
REVIEWING THE SITUATION

If you were the parent, how might you react to this letter? From whose point of view was the letter written? Jot down your reactions. What did the principal do well? What would you do differently? Did the principal address the issues raised by the parent? How *sensitive* was this letter to the parent viewpoint?

CREATING A FAVORABLE IMPRESSION

School principals often need to write messages that give bad news. As the writer of the "bad news" memo or letter they need to be aware of the *feelings* of the parent as well as maintain a professional tone. However, the one thing we have observed when administrators write to parents is this: It usually lacks SENSITIVITY to the parents' perspective. Here's a checklist for you to consider when writing to parents.

FIGURE 4.2. AUDIENCE ANALYSIS CHECKLIST

- Jot down your purpose.
  - What do you want to happen?
  - What is it you want the parent to do or think?
- What do you know about parents?
  - What kind of information will they accept?
  - How much information do they need?
- What tone do you want to convey?
  - Authoritative, Collaborative, Friendly, Supportive, Objective?
- What is the attitude of the parent?
  - Positive, Negative, Neutral?
- What form of communication is needed?
  - Letter, Note, Phone Call?

WRITING BAD NEWS

We know how stressful it is to deal with student discipline and upset parents, particularly when the problems keep coming. However, we also know that parent support is crucial in creating and maintaining open lines of communication. Here's a suggested format that will help you to write bad news letters quickly and sensitively.

Issue: Student tardiness to class

- **If possible, begin the letter by noting something positive about the student's behavior or situation.** Parents need a "buffer" statement that builds a bridge between you and them. They need to feel that their child will receive help and that there is hope for success. Example: *Brian is a good student and his school record up to now has been exemplary.*

- **Present what needs to change.** Example: *I am concerned that he has been late to class three times this week without any reasonable excuse.*
- **Explain the reason for the action you are taking.** Example: *I have reminded him of the rules and policies outlined in the student handbook concerning tardiness to class and advised him to follow these guidelines.*
- **Indicate the desired behavior you seek.** Example: *I expect Brian to be prompt for all of his classes*
- **Offer assistance in achieving compliance.** Example: *I told Brian that if there is a specific problem preventing his prompt arrival to class, he needs to see me to discuss possible solutions and alternatives.*
- **Describe future consequences.** Example: *If he continues to be tardy, I will have to keep him for after school detention.*
- **Offer hope and encouragement.** Example: *Incidents such as these are always upsetting to parents. Please speak to Brian about this matter. We have confidence in Brian and know that he will continue to make decisions in his best interest.*

FIGURE 4.3. WRITING BAD NEWS

Dear Mr. and Mrs. Marino:	**Document Analysis**
John has missed 15 unexcused days of school this semester and I am writing you to express my concern. His academic success is directly related to school attendance. John's number of absences has already affected his math and English performance when he missed two mid-semester exams.	States problem and what needs to change.
Because of the excessive number of unexcused absences, in the future John must bring in a doctor's statement for each day missed. Furthermore, I am asking that you make an appointment within the next five days with Mr. Han-	States reason for action taken.

son, John's guidance counselor. I will be present at this meeting.

It is my hope that we will be able to resolve this matter and work out a mutually agreeable solution. Consequences for continued unexcused absences will unfortunately result in beginning due process procedures leading to expulsion from Walton High School.

Offers assistance in a collaborative tone.

Describes future consequences.

Thank you for your prompt attention to this matter. John is a good student and we want him to make decisions in his best interest.

Offers encouragement.

Exercise 4.2
BREAKING BAD NEWS

Directions: Using this format and the Audience Analysis Checklist, rewrite the follow-up conference letter to Mrs. Clough.

SIZING UP ATTITUDE

How does the attitude of the parent guide your planning of the written document? How will these attitudes affect what and how you write to these individuals? Let's see how the attitude of the reader might change the tone, the amount of information, and the organizational approach you select.

Here's the situation. Your school community is experiencing growth. Enrollment is higher than projected and you have to add another fifth grade classroom. This means moving students from the existing two classes.

- Jot down your PURPOSE. What is it you want the parent to do or think?
- Consider the ATTITUDE of the parent. Is the parent's attitude toward you or the school neutral, positive, or negative?
- Jot down the TYPES of INFORMATION parents need to know based on ATTITUDE.
- Decide upon an ORGANIZATIONAL STRATEGY using one or more of the following approaches:

FIGURE 4.4. ORGANIZATIONAL PATTERNS

• Chronological Order	Discuss the process or plan in sequential order.
• Topic Order	Arrange the key points by preference.
• Need-Plan- Benefit	Identify the need, provide a plan, and cite the benefits.
• Comparative Advantages	Present two alternatives and then recommend one.
• Cause and Effect	Describe a situation and then present the effects or consequences.
• Problem-Solution	Introduce problem and possible solutions to resolve the issue.
• Question-Answer	Raise the issue and then respond.
• Analytic Approach	State a problem, your analysis, and solution.
• Inductive Approach	Furnish facts and findings before conclusions.
• Deductive Approach	Start with a short summary of conclusions and follow with facts.

Here are three letters written to parents concerning this issue. Each considers the attitude of the parent from a different viewpoint and selects an organizational strategy to get the message across in a clear, concise, and sensitive way. Within a letter or writing document, you may use more than one strategy.

FIGURE 4.5. PARENT IS NEUTRAL
PURPOSE: TO INFORM PARENT ABOUT CHANGE IN TEACHER
TONE: OBJECTIVE
STRATEGY: PROBLEM-SOLUTION

	Document Analysis
Dear Mr. and Mrs. Jones: Springville Elementary has experienced an increase in the number of students who have joined our school family. We now have enough students to provide an additional fifth grade class to our upper elementary division. By adding this class we can lower the student-teacher ratio in all of our fifth grade classes and	Describes the problem situation. Emphasizes the benefit to parent and student.

therefore give more individual attention to our students.

Moving students is always a difficult task especially when school has started and students have established their routines. However, the teachers and administrative staff have carefully reviewed the situation and developed a process that we feel is fair for all involved. Given specific criteria, each student was reviewed for possible placement in the new fifth grade class.

Expresses empathy. Shows this action has been thoughtfully planned.

Your child, Elizabeth, has been recommended for placement in the new fifth grade class. Mrs. Bowden, the newly employed teacher, is a highly recommended teacher and offers five years of successful teaching experience with fourth and fifth grade students. You are invited to contact your child's current teacher for specific information regarding Elizabeth's placement recommendation. A general meeting has been scheduled for Monday, October 16, at 6:30 p.m. in the school library for parents of students who will be making this change.

States action taken.

Assures parent of teacher qualifications.

Provides a communication channel for questions, concerns, and feedback.

We are concerned about your child's reaction to this change. If questions or concerns arise after Elizabeth's placement with Mrs. Bowden, please do not hesitate to call me.

Offers help if problems develop.

FIGURE 4.6. PARENT IS POSITIVE
TONE: FRIENDLY
STRATEGY: INDUCTIVE APPROACH

Dear Mr. and Mrs. Gibson:

Document Analysis

As you know from our monthly PTA Advisory Meetings, Springville is experiencing rapid growth due to our increase

Acknowledges a current working relationship.

in district population. As a result we have the opportunity to add another fifth grade class to our upper elementary division.	Presents the facts.
Moving students is always a difficult task after the school year has started. However, we feel the overall benefit in reducing class size in all the fifth grade classes will offset the initial discomfort for all involved. The teachers and the administrative staff have carefully reviewed each student's potential for success for placement in the new class.	Expresses sensitivity to the situation. Indicates each student was considered.
Courtney has been recommended by her teacher as a student who will benefit by this change. She is an independent learner, enjoys new challenges, and her learning style is compatible with the teaching style of the newly employed fifth grade teacher, Mrs. Bowden —who comes to us with excellent teaching credentials and recommendations.	States recommendation. Stresses the benefit to student.
You have been and continue to be strong supporters of our school. A general meeting for parents of students involved in this enrollment change has been scheduled for Monday, October 16, at 6:30 p.m. in the school library. If this decision causes you any concern or if questions develop, please don't hesitate to call me.	Acknowledges parent support. Provides communication channel for feedback. Offers assistance.

FIGURE 4.7. PARENT IS NEGATIVE
STRATEGY: PROBLEM SOLUTION/CHRONOLOGICAL
TONE: AUTHORITATIVE

Dear Mrs. Long:	**Document Analysis**
Springville Elementary is experiencing rapid population growth in the community. As a result, our student enrollment	States problem situation.

has increased student numbers in all our classrooms. However, student registration in the fifth grade has expanded enough for us to add another class to our upper elementary division. This will significantly reduce the student-teacher ratio for all fifth grade classes.

Indicates solution. Emphasizes benefit to students.

Moving students is never an easy task, especially when school has already started and our students have established daily routines. However, we have developed a fair and equitable process for moving students.

Shows sensitivity to situation.

Indicates plan.

First, teachers reviewed all students for potential success in the new fifth grade classroom. Then, the names of those students recommended were numerically placed on a list by gender and then randomly selected. Finally, our counselor reviewed each fifth grade class list to ensure that each reflected academic, social, cultural, and gender balance.

Outlines specific steps taken to identify students for change to new classroom. The writer's purpose is to reassure parents the process is objective.

Your child, Mark, has been recommended for the new fifth grade class. You are invited to contact your child's current teacher for specific information about this placement decision. A general parent meeting has been scheduled for parents of students involved in this change. We will meet on Monday, October 16, at 6:30 p.m. in the school library.

States placement decision.

Provides communication channel for feedback.

If you have any questions or concerns, please do not hesitate to call me.

Offers assistance.

What do you like best or least about these examples? What would you change?

Exercise 4.3
AUDIENCE ANALYSIS

Locate a letter you have written to a parent or parents concerning a difficult topic or problem. Reassess your approach based on PURPOSE, PARENT ATTITUDE, and ORGANIZATIONAL APPROACH. Then rewrite the letter. How is your second letter different from the first? Ask a colleague to give you feedback on both examples.

REWORDING FOR POSITIVE IMPACT

Remember what we said earlier? The one thing every parent wants to know is: How is my child performing? What you write and how you write it are taken very seriously and very personally by a parent. If there is the slightest perception that the school is "out to get" his or her child, the attitude of the parent will be defensive, negative, and non-supporting.

The following are examples of rewording sentences to place the emphasis on the parent's point of view rather than on your point of view:

- **Principal's Point of View**: *I am happy to inform you that your son has....*
- **Parent's Point of View**: *Your son, Blake, has significantly increased his skill in....*

Suggestion: Shift the focus from the administrator viewpoint to the parent viewpoint. Who is it they are most interested in knowing about?

- **Principal's Point of View**: *We require each student to have a parent signature on the daily agenda.*
- **Parent's Point of View**: *To assist your child in completing homework, a parent must sign the daily agenda notebook.*

Suggestion: A brief reason for a specific requirement addressing the benefit to the student may encourage more support.

Exercise 4.4
REWORDING FOR MORE POSITIVE IMPACT

Locate five to ten letters you have written to parents. Highlight all the sentences that use the *I* pronoun—(Principal's Viewpoint). Now rewrite these sentences using the Parent's Viewpoint and read them aloud. Have a parent give you feedback on your before and after letters.

SUMMARY

Investigations and observations about administrators' writing show that writing appropriately for different audiences and demonstrating sensitivity to the reader's point of view is not consistently performed by principals. Principals, in general, do not acknowledge an understanding of the reader's problem or empathize with the individual in their writing. Sensitivity in letters to parents is particularly not evident (Podsen, 1991). Generally, because of the subject and the seriousness of disciplinary matters, their tone is courteous but restrained. Such letters must include what the parent needs to know, especially when it pertains to students' rights. We know that suspension and expulsion issues cannot be taken lightly. However, we would like you to consider that a brief statement showing empathy or understanding of the parent's position may go far in helping to build collaborative communication channels.

As writers we have the responsibility to "communicate the message and make sure it is easy for the reader "(Yerkes and Morgan, 1991). To do this we must:

- Know the audience.
- Choose words the audience understands.
- Tell them what they want to know.
- Be sensitive.
- Encourage two-way communication.
- Be specific.
- Be organized, clear, and friendly.
- Consider their viewpoint.

RESOURCES

BOOKS AND ARTICLES

Title: *People Skills*
Author: Robert Bolton
Publisher: Touchstone Books, 1986

This book provides practical tips and ideas for asserting yourself, listening to others, resolving conflicts, and collaborating to solve problems.

Title: *School Administrator's Complete Letter Book*
Author: Gerald Tomlinson
Publisher: Prentice Hall, 1984

More than 100 memos and letters written to parents, teachers, students, other school administrators, business people, and the community at large. This resource guide deals with issues faced by school principals and the types of writing demanded on the job. Each writing document responds to a specific need in a courteous, thoughtful, and professional manner.

SEMINARS AND WORKSHOPS

The workshops and seminars listed in this guide were chosen for their appeal to school administrators. Since the publication of this text, some seminars may have been upgraded or replaced and others may no longer be offered. Similarly, costs and locations may have also changed. We recommend that you contact the consulting group directly for current information and availability.

Title: *The Sensitive Leader*
Consulting Group: National Association of Secondary School Principals
Contact Number: Tel: 703-860-0200

A developmental workshop designed to enhance the principal's ability to assess the needs, perceptions, and viewpoints of different audiences within the school community and to respond in a way that empowers people and builds relationships.

Title: *From the Desk of... A Written Communication Program for School Administrators*
Consulting Group: National Association of Secondary School Principals
Contact Number: Tel: 703-860-0200

A developmental program that engages participants in multiple writing tasks based on the job demands in the principalship. Instructional techniques foster building open communication techniques within school settings.

Title: *Conflict Analysis and Resolution*
Consulting Group: National Association of Secondary School Principals
Contact Number: Tel: 703-860-0200

A developmental workshop that teaches principals how to assess their current approach to resolving conflict and developing strategies for dealing with conflict situations in schools.

Title: *Managing Differences and Agreements: Making Conflict Work for You*
Consulting Group: Designed Learning, Inc.
Contact Number: Tel: 908-754-5102

This seminar presents effective strategies to help managers deal with people who are angry, emotional, or irrational. Participants develop skills for handling situations where conflict may be caused by time pressures and differences over performance.

CHAPTER REFERENCES

Pawlas, G. (1995). *The administrator's guide to school community relations*. Princeton, NJ: Eye On Education.

Podsen, I.J. (February, 1991). Apprehension and effective writing in the principalship. *NASSP Bulletin*, 89-96.

Yerkes, D., and Morgan, S. (1991). *Strategies for success: An administrator's guide to writing*. Reston, VA: National Association of Secondary School Principals.

Vann, A. (1992). Ten ways to improve principal-parent communication. *Principal*, 30-31.

5

Writing to Central Office Staff

"Contrary to general belief, writing isn't something that only 'writers' do: writing is a basic skill for getting through life. Writing is thinking on paper..."

—Unknown

Do you find yourself becoming apprehensive when faced with writing to a central office staff member, much less the superintendent? If so, you're not alone. Getting our thoughts organized and written in a manner that truly communicates is not an easy task!

Most of us don't relish the thought of writing to the Superintendent, the Assistant Superintendent, or to any number of other staff members at the central level. We agonize over what to say, and how to say it in written form. Our letters, memos, and reports, according to Roddick (1984), should "communicate to the reader in a direct and accessible way." Our task becomes even more troublesome when, as Roddick suggests, we create a product more for ourselves than for the reader. When this happens, we violate many of the rules for effective writing.

We believe that clever school principals work continuously to improve their relationship with the school district office. This relationship will often be stronger through an understanding of what is taking place in the school and the school's community. Very few superintendents or district staff members have the opportunity to hear all of the good news about your school first-hand. It's imperative for today's school leader to skillfully translate the good news, and sometimes the bad, into a written form that is clear, concise, and constructive.

Knowing when and how to write to central level staff is a combination of art and science. By artistry, we mean knowing what is expected, and what is not, in your school district. Some superintendents prefer brief, executive summary highlights, while others may want detailed, full narrative reports. Discovering what is expected is up to you. The science comes through the methodology of the writing process. Whether your district staff wants a little or a lot, clear and correct writing is critical to your success.

CLARIFYING YOUR PURPOSE

William Zinsser (1985) may have said it best when he wrote, "Clutter is the disease of American writing. We are a society strangling in unnecessary words, circular constructions, pompous frills and meaningless jargon." How often have you read a memo or a letter and wondered aloud, "What does this mean?" Every profession has its clichés, jargon, and babble. Use of these tend to confuse the reader as to the real purpose for our writing. Right or wrong, we are often accused of having more than our share of these problems and consequently being less than clear in our writing.

By thinking more plainly about why and to whom you are writing, you can begin the process of writing more effectively. The process of writing to district level staff is much like planning a trip. You need to decide a destination before your plan has much meaning. What do you want to accomplish? Is it to inform someone of an upcoming event? Is it to describe the success of a particular program within your school? Posing questions such as these will allow you to become more specific and less cluttered with your correspondence. Once you know where you are going you're more likely to know when you have arrived.

Clarifying your purpose in writing to central office staff is easier when you decide the intent. Writing a statement of purpose is a simple way to think about the destination you hope to reach. Consider each of the following sentence beginnings and finish them in your own words:

I INTEND TO

- show how…
- convince my reader that…

- discuss the reasons why...
- explain why...
- prove that...
- compare...

You may have several reasons for writing to central office staff. Keep in mind that you cannot and should not try to address all of your reasons in one memo, letter, or report. Sticking with one topic is more likely to fulfill your original purpose. And, regardless of how much you may have to say, remember it is the clear, concise, and specific message that gets read. Superintendents and their staff are just as busy as you are in keeping up with day-to-day business. No one needs, or looks forward to, reading long, rambling, and sometimes incoherent messages. Here is a checklist to guide you in assessing your purpose:

___ I intend to give **information**.
___ I intend to give information and an **evaluation** or assessment of a situation at my school.
___ I intend to give information, an evaluation/assessment, and offer **conclusions** about a situation or event at my school.
___ I intend to give information, an evaluation, offer conclusions, and make **recommendations** about a situation or event at my school.

Using a checklist such as this will help guide you in clarifying your purpose for writing. Roddick (1984) recommends the use of these four basic kinds of reports (information, evaluation, conclusion, and recommendation) as a means to streamline report writing. She states, and we agree, that the goal is to "...convey all the necessary information directly to readers without confusion or irrelevancies."

Another way of clarifying your purpose in writing is to consider the organization of the message. Organizing your writing is as simple as asking the Five W's and the H (Who, What, When, Where, Why, and How).

THE FIVE W'S AND THE H

Who

- Who will be reading this?
- Who else might be interested in reading this?

What

- What form of communication is best? Memo, Letter, Note, Report?
- What should be included?
- What do you hope to accomplish with your message?
- What will the attitude of the reader be?

When

- When did/or will an event take place?
- When do you want action or a response?
- When will more information/direction be available?

Where

- Where do you hope to go with your message?
- Where can more information/direction be obtained?

Why

- Why should anyone, especially the reader, be interested?
- Why do you need more information or direction?

How

- How can the reader help you?
- How much information/direction do you need?
- How can the reader address your purpose in writing to them?

Newspaper journalists typically use this approach to writing organization. Their message must relate the key facts in a concise, clear, and coherent manner. When we follow their lead in organizing our thoughts, our purpose quickly becomes evident to the reader. Our goal is achieved, let the reader know what to expect!

APPRAISING AUDIENCE NEEDS

Clarifying your purpose helps to focus your ideas and decide exactly what it is you want to accomplish. The next question becomes, who is my audience? When you plan letters, memos, and reports, it's critically important to keep in mind the viewpoints of the reader.

We've already explored the notion that superintendents and other central office staff have busy schedules and many demands. Unless you're blessed with an unusually attentive central office staff who are voracious readers, you might consider these questions:

- What is the background of my reader and how does that relate to my proposed correspondence?
- Am I only writing to this one person? Are there others who will be interested?
- What kind of reaction is likely from the reader?
- What typically happens to correspondence such as mine? Is it shared with a few, or many? Is it possible the board of education will see this?
- Will the reader be left with a positive image of me and my school?

Posing and answering these types of questions should guide you in considering the needs of your reader. Earlier, we introduced the idea that writing to central office staff is both an art and a science. If you know your superintendent prefers a bullet format for memos and reports, does it make much sense to send a two-page narrative on why your school needs an additional staff member? We don't think so either, especially now that we know what the audience wants and needs.

Exercise 5.1
CENTRAL OFFICE CORRESPONDENCE

Take a look at your memos and letters to your system level colleagues. Find at least two and review them using the 5 W's and H as a guide to check for clarity, conciseness, and an organizational strategy. Ask a colleague at the central office to give you feedback on your writing. Remember, no news may not necessarily be good news on your writing effectiveness.

KEEPING YOUR SUPERINTENDENT INFORMED

We can all relate to the question, "Why didn't you tell me?" Sometimes superintendents are surprised when a school board member or a member of the news media asks about a situation about which the superintendent has little or no information. The superintendent correctly asks, "Why didn't I know this?"

Communication and counseling experts agree that the basic

foundation for common understanding is clear communication. Do you believe your success as a principal, or the success of your school, is even remotely linked to the superintendent? If the answer is yes, you'll find yourself looking for ways to communicate more precisely with your superintendent. Often this can be accomplished by writing the superintendent a well-constructed and clear memo or letter. The resulting improved relationship changes the focus of the question from "Why didn't you…?" to "Tell me more."

A superintendent needs to know what's happening in your school and community. It only makes sense that the more clear and specific information you provide, the more likely it can be translated in the way you desire, leaving little room for others to interpret. Don't wait for the board member or the news media to give their own unique twist to information. Provide the information up front to your superintendent and know exactly what has been transmitted for the record. We know of few, if any, superintendents who are clairvoyant! Keep superintendents informed of important events and situations and you won't have to rely on their supernatural skills!

Keeping the superintendent informed requires your constant attention. You demonstrate good judgment and communication skills when you provide information to the most influential school administrator in your district. Although many districts have informational specialists on staff, don't assume your story, or the story of your school, will always be at the forefront of the superintendent's mind. A communication matrix for keeping the superintendent informed may help you in maintaining that constant attention (Figure 5.1).

Add to the information provided in the matrix and develop additional topics that you consider important for the superintendent to know about you, your school, your students and staff, and your school community.

When keeping the superintendent informed, keep these tips in mind:

- If given a choice, be brief.
- Be direct and clear.
- State your purpose clearly and early in your communication.
- Remember that others, including board members or

FIGURE 5.1. DOES THE SUPERINTENDENT KNOW?

TOPIC	TYPE OF INFORMATION	WAYS TO INFORM
STUDENTS	Demographics	Reports/Graphs/Charts
	Awards/Success	Letters/Memos/Graphs
		Charts/News Releases
		Award Certificates
	Problems	Reports/Graphs/Charts
		Letters/Memos
STAFF	Demographics	Reports/Graphs/Charts
		Tables
	Awards/Success	Letters/Memos/Graphs
	Achievements	Charts/News Releases
		Newsletters /Award
		Certificates
	Problems	Chronological Reports
		Letters/Memos Evaluations
		Records/Notes
SCHOOL COMMUNITY	Demographics	Reports/Graphs/Charts
	Interests/Concerns	Letters/Memos/Reports
		Newsletters/Bulletins
SCHOOL FACILITIES	Usage	Letters/Memos/Graphs
		Charts
	Needs	Letters/Memos/Reports
OTHER TOPICS		

the news media, may read what you have written.

- The superintendent is the most influential school administrator in your district.
- Avoid casual comments.
- Back up your points with data or with clear persuasive information.
- Avoid carelessness in your writing.
- Present your writing in the proper format.
- Pay attention to detail and appearance.

Here's an example of a memo from a principal to her superintendent. We think it demonstrates most of the tips listed above. What do you think?

FIGURE 5.2. MEMO TO SUPERINTENDENT

A sudden increase in long-distance phone calls from a high school prompted questions from the district office. Here is the principal's reply:

Document Analysis

DATE: December 10, 199_

TO: Cliff Bennett, Superintendent
FROM: Sherry Robinson, Principal
SUBJECT: Long-Distance Phone Bills

Based on our conversation regarding the phone bills for October and November, I reviewed the billing statements for these months. I concluded that most of the bills were incurred in connection with four student activities at our high school.

Analyze this memo.

1. New Band Uniforms. The greatest number of calls came from our Music Department concerning our new band uniforms. We have not been able to reach an agreement with Dalton Mills of Los Angeles, California, on pricing and delivery. These calls were necessary to negotiate these details and bring us closer to a mutual agreement. I expect this problem to be resolved within the next week; thus the calls to Los Angeles will end.

Identify what the writer has done well.

2. Tennis Tournament. Our school is hosting the USTA Regional Girls Tennis Tournament. The phone calls for this event totaled $55.00 and will be reimbursed by the USTA regional office.

3. Dance Team Competition. A number of phone calls were made in regard to our jazz team's participation in the upcoming state competition. These calls were necessary to finalize travel plans and to discuss logistical matters. Further calls will be needed to coordinate lodging for team members and chaperones.

4. Regional All-State Basketball Tryouts. Our school is serving as sponsors for the state basketball tryouts. The phone calls for this event will be reimbursed by our booster club.

I hope this memo clarifies the matter of the high school's large phone bills for the months in question. We do have many student activities and programs that require long-distance communication, but we also realize the need to keep these calls to a minimum. We will continue to monitor our calls to accomplish this goal.

If I can be of further assistance, please let me know.

Evaluating Your Communication with Your Supervisor

Almost everyone wants to be perceived by others in the most positive ways. You like to know that you're doing a good job and you especially want to know that from your boss. At least one way to evaluate your effectiveness is to evaluate your communication with your supervisor. Has the boss told you lately, in writing, that you're doing a good job? Have you told your supervisor, in writing, what you're doing and why? If the answer to either of these questions is "No" consider the following:

- I routinely send copies of letters of appreciation and thanks about me, my school, my staff, or my students to my supervisor.
- I routinely send a copy of my calendar to my supervisor so he/she will have a better understanding of my schedule.
- I communicate with my supervisor about emerging

problems with students, staff, or community.

- I maintain anecdotal or chronological accounts of situations that may involve my supervisor (examples: severe student discipline issues, emerging staff problems, etc.).
- I send copies of my school newsletter/bulletin on a regular basis to my supervisor.

Every principal can relate to the problems he or she encounters when a situation is emerging in the classroom or community and the principal has little or no information. Your supervisors are no different from you! They want and need information that will enable them to be prepared to help you when the time arises. Your job is to supply that information through regular communication.

Exercise 5.2
SUPERINTENDENT-PRINCIPAL COMMUNICATIONS

We mentioned in this chapter that superintendents may differ in the amount of information they need from you and the degree to which they wish to be consulted on decisions. However, we know that most superintendents frown on surprises. Here is an exercise to help you assess your communication effectiveness with the BOSS. Circle YES or NO depending on your response to the descriptor.

1. Your superintendent understands your job responsibilities, needs, and problems.	1. **YES** **NO**
2. You know your job duties and responsibilities from an up-to-date written job description.	2. **YES** **NO**
3. Your superintendent is interested in you as a person as well as a professional.	3. **YES** **NO**
4. You understand the target dates and deadlines for meeting school goals and routine job assignments.	4. **YES** **NO**
5. You show integrity and keep your word.	5. **YES** **NO**
6. You are approachable and available when needed by the superintendent.	6. **YES** **NO.**
7. You view communication as important and give adequate time to complete writing products on time.	7. **YES** **NO**
8. Your communication style is collegial and cooperative rather than authoritative or defensive.	8. **YES** **NO.**
9. You express yourself clearly and tactfully when problems and concerns arise.	9. **YES** **NO**
10. You strive to understand the superintendent and to be understood by him or her.	10. **YES** **NO**

11. You are candid with your superintendent.	11. **YES**	NO
12. You avoid being judgmental and jumping to conclusions when the superintendent contacts you.	12. **YES**	NO
13. You know the kinds of information your superintendent is most interested in getting from you.	13. **YES**	NO
14. You have a clear idea on the amount of information your superintendent needs to keep informed and to make important decision..	14. **YES**	NO
15. You don't assume your superintendent lacks interest in most of what goes on in your school.	**15. YES**	NO
16. You make sure you give your superintendent any bad news.	**16. YES**	NO
17. You don't wait for your superintendent to make a decision before voicing recommendations.	**17. YES**	NO
18. You communicate with the superintendent regularly rather than only at his or her request.	**18. YES**	NO.

Summarized from NASSP Practitioner, *Assessing the Communications Effectiveness of Your School.* Vol. XVII, No.2, December 1990. Reprinted with permission

SUMMARY AND TIPS

This chapter begins by introducing the idea that most of us are somewhat apprehensive when faced with writing to a central office staff member. Careful thinking about purpose, organization, and when and how to write may reduce that fear. The following tips may help you when preparing to write to this audience:

- List the key central office staff upon whom your success depends. Keep them informed.
- Check with your superintendent about any surprises in your area. Look for ways to avoid any recurrences.
- Don't gloss over anything that goes wrong. Report the situation ASAP.
- Request a meeting with your superintendent to discuss mutual expectations. Clarify the level of authority your superintendent expects. Keep him or her informed.
- State your purpose for writing clearly, concisely and as coherently as possible.
- Write for the reader's understanding.

- State your points candidly, completely, and convincingly.
- Double check all correspondence for accuracy, form and function.

RESOURCES

BOOKS AND ARTICLES

Title: *Written Communications and the School Administrator*
Author: Audrey Joyce
Publisher: Allyn & Bacon, 1991

No matter what the situation, good or bad, as an administrator you've got to write well. The author gives practical writing instruction in an easy to grasp way. The book contains over 100 sample letters arranged by purpose and audience.

Title: *School Administrator's Complete Letter Book*
Author: Gerald Tomlinson
Publisher: Prentice Hall, 1984

More than 100 memos and letters written to parents, teachers, students, other school administrators, business people, and the community at large. This resource guide deals with issues faced by school principals and the types of writing demanded on the job. Each writing document responds to a specific need in a courteous, thoughtful, and professional manner.

SEMINARS AND WORKSHOPS

The workshops and seminars listed in this guide were chosen for their appeal to school administrators. Since the publication of this text, some seminars may have been upgraded or replaced and others may no longer be offered. Similarly, costs and locations may have also changed. We recommend that you contact the consulting group directly for current information and availability.

Title: *From the Desk Of... A Written Communication Program for School Administrators*
Consulting Group: National Association of Secondary School Principals
Contact Number: Tel: 703-860-0200

A developmental program that engages participants in multiple writing tasks based on the job demands in the principalship. Instructional techniques foster building open communication techniques within school settings.

CHAPTER REFERENCES

Roddick, E. (1984). *Writing that means business: A manager's guide.* New York: Macmillan.

Strunk, W., Jr., & White, E. B. (1979). *The elements of style* (3rd ed.). New York: Macmillan.

Zinsser, W. (1985). *On writing well* (3rd ed.). New York: Harper & Row.

6

Writing to Your Peers

"Being a writer is essentially a life full of homework... only it's impossible to write it the night before it's due."
—Fran Lebowitz

Imitation: The Greatest Compliment

"How can I ever keep up with all of this paperwork? Who has the time to write all of these memos? Don't they know what it is like in the trenches? How can I ever create all of the writing requested of me?"

The school leader today needs to write on an ever-growing demanding basis with less time to do it. One of the keys to better time management and production is to write to your peers. How can additional writing create less writing? When administrators share their written communications, the burden for creativity and production rests on the shoulders of many rather than a few.

There is a myth in education that every individual administrator must create all of his or her own newsletters, memos, proposals, curriculum guides, budget justifications, and the entire myriad of written communications that are expected. If administrators share with their peers, they will find that the collective efforts are greater and more creative than the efforts of a lonely leader working late into the night. When administrators share their writing products with peers, ***imitation***, the greatest form of flattery, is free to operate.

Why write an article on school closings during inclement weather when a colleague has written a perfect one? And that colleague, in turn, may use your article on the effects of television watching on the quality of homework. If every school wishes to buy an analog-digital monitor to improve the teaching of computer programs, why should eleven principals take the time to write eleven different but similar proposals? Budget proposals are completed with greater speed and expertise when administrators share their writing with peers.

Principals, Assistant Principals, Academic Directors, Chairpersons, and Central Office staff benefit greatly when they communicate in writing with their peers. When the lines of communication are open, the administrator's job becomes more proficient and the perception of the office is enhanced. This chapter provides the framework for improved peer writing.

PINNING DOWN YOUR PURPOSE

Throughout this guide we have stressed (perhaps harped on) this point: Adult writers in leadership positions often show problems in successfully communicating the purpose of their written messages. This theme surfaces in every chapter dealing with audience. Let's look at eight reasons for writing to our peers.

- **Information.** A strange car has been seen on several occasions near the school and your colleagues in surrounding schools need the information. Or, an excellent speaker on a current topic is coming to the area so the information is shared with peers.
- **Persuasion.** You wish to have the district purchase a particular item or establish a new curriculum and you need the support of your fellow principals.
- **Congratulations.** Another school has an outstanding program that sincerely needs to be recognized. A recognition from a colleague is one of the highest compliments paid.
- **Sympathy.** A colleague has a personal loss or a tragedy strikes the school of another principal. A quick personal note is greatly appreciated.
- **Request.** You need information, the use of a building, assistance on a project, or a change in schedule for a shared teacher.
- **Administrative Practice.** A report from a worthwhile

conference or a summary of a pilot program is sent to peers. Or, a copy of a report is sent to the Central Office which would impact a colleague's school.

- **Feedback.** The critiquing and sharing of written materials with a trusted colleague.
- **Circulation.** Written materials are critiqued and shared with fellow principals such as newsletters, parenting notices, programs for plays and music presentations, and instructional articles.

CALCULATING PEER RELATIONS

Positive, productive communications with peers are important to ensure that you get the support and the information you need to do your job well. "How open are you and your peers to communication exchanges?" Part of the problem in communicating with colleagues may be that your peer relations are more competitive than cooperative.

Let's take a "fresh look" at this topic. Have you considered the fact that one or more of your peers may become your BOSS in the future? What do your colleagues think of you? Are your relationships collegial (providing ongoing coaching) or adversarial (getting ahead by holding back information and support)? Coaching is one of the best ways to help peers grow.

When should a principal write to peers? By assessing your attitude and the attitude of your colleagues the answers are clearer. The need becomes apparent as communication exchanges begin to reap the benefits for individual administrators.

START BY DOING

Fostering better peer communication means being attentive to and interested in others. The only way to begin is to begin. Start by sending copies of written materials that are beneficial to colleagues. A copy of a monthly newsletter sent to parents will spark interest and give ideas. Attach a note that gives the reader permission to use any article or request a copy of the newsletter. When the flow of information begins, add copies of other materials that are helpful (i.e., a testing schedule, a code of conduct, a letter of recommendation (with name omitted), and a suspension letter).

KNOW YOUR AUDIENCE

Realize that your audience is someone just like you. This audience doesn't want to waste time on boastful and jargon-laded material. Their time is precious and they are constantly in search of useful materials. This is a group that is looking for practical and useful written communications.

TO WRITE OR NOT TO WRITE

Whether to write or to use another method of communication is an all-important question based on time management and the needs of your audience. There are times when it is better to use the telephone or a face-to-face meeting to convey a message. A written document, including electronic mail, is irrevocable. Written communications take time if they are properly prepared so the time spent must be worth the benefit of the product. Your colleagues will always read and respect your sharing of written communications if the writing products are pertinent and easy to read and digest.

BE POSITIVE

A positive relationship among colleagues who are sharing their writing is a key ingredient in fostering future communication. Resist all temptations to critique a peer's writing in any way, shape, or form. One negative comment will instantly destroy the trust level necessary for open communication. Giving positive feedback is a powerful motivator when it is specific and behavioral. When giving feedback consider these tips:

- Accurately describe the behavior.
- Point out the impact of the behavior or performance on you, the job, or the school district.
- Emphasize the behavior you will imitate.
- Reinforce these behaviors as often as possible.

KEEPING THE INFORMATION FLOW MOVING

Writing to peers is only as effective as the regular flow of information. Interest wanes in all areas of education administration unless a concentrated effort is made. There are always distractions lurking behind every turn to take a principal from the important to the thing of the moment or the promise of something new. To keep the information in motion administrators must:

- Set up a routine with secretaries and peers for certain materials to be distributed routinely after publication, i.e., newsletters, calendars, programs, etc.
- Set aside time each day, with the door closed, to write. Better yet, find a place in the media center or a conference room where only your secretary knows where to find you.
- Always be on the prowl for materials to share with peers.
- Always encourage the efforts made by all administrators involved in the sharing. Send short positive notes complimenting peers' efforts.
- Be an initiator by introducing new forms of writing that have not been shared. Put your neck out by distributing a letter of reprimand with names deleted.

Exercise 6.1
PEER EXCHANGE CHECKLIST

Listed below is a checklist to help you and your peers keep a record of the types of written communications which are distributed. Feel free to add and improve on this inventory as the shared writings become more diversified.

- I send letters of congratulations to my peers.
- I send sympathy notes to colleagues.
- I send copies of school newsletters to colleagues.
- I send copies of conference reports to peers.
- I send copies of parent handbooks to colleagues.
- I send copies of course proposals to peers.
- I share my budget justifications with peers.
- I share my daily memos with colleagues.
- I positively accept comments made concerning my writing.

- I request that colleagues send me examples of written communication.
- I am willing to ask a colleague to proofread my written work.
- I spend time each day practicing the skill of writing.
- I send short complimentary notes to peers on their writing products.
- I don't write in anger.
- I always keep my audience in mind.
- I keep my writing brief and concise.

WRITING EXHIBITS

The writing samples that follow serve as examples and as frameworks for peer communication. They are not meant to be perfect but to provide a place to begin the writing process. Yes, it's OK to use humor. Perhaps with peers most of all we can let our hair down (what's left) and share some "off-the-wall moments." Laughter is the best medicine.

FIGURE 6.1. TO INFORM

To: Comrades in Arms
From: Fighting Jane
Date: December 15
Re: Important Dates for Sunset High

The week of March 10th is an important time at our high school. We have set aside the week as college and career week. We are expecting high parent participation during the school day and at night.

I request that the elementary and middle school not schedule any parent meetings that would create a conflict for parents. If there is a problem with any of those dates, please give me a call, so we can discuss changes that could accommodate both. The schedule for the event will be finalized on January 10th.

Thanks for the help. I owe you one, or is it two, or maybe three. Who keeps count?

FIGURE 6.2. TO PERSUADE

To: Harry Moneybags
From: Poor John
Re: Budget Justification—Item 26—Library Books

The Weareneedy Elementary School is requesting $3,000.00 for new library books for the next school year. There have been no moneys allocated in this code for the past two school years. The requested amount would allow us to bring the library back to the level it was two years ago.

As you are aware from your recent visit, our library books are in constant use. The local public library is a great distance from the homes of our students so our school is the main source of books for our children. Our large circulation contributes to a number of titles being lost each year and accelerates normal wear and tear. The popular books are in constant circulation. Our collection now totals 7,500 compared to 7,850 two years ago. We need to replenish the collection before it becomes too expensive. We have taken extraordinary precautions to keep loss and wear and tear at a minimum.

This budget item is needed to foster an educational program which depends on the regular circulation of reading and research materials. Your help is greatly appreciated.

FIGURE 6.3. TO INSTRUCT

To: Heather Frazzled
From: Peggy Experienced
Re: Your Request on Parent-Teacher Conferences

As I promised, attached are copies of all of the materials that are used to schedule and arrange parent-teacher conferences. The dates on each of the memos and letters will give you a timeline to follow for distribution.

The school of hard knocks, better known as experience, has taught me the following:

- Discuss the entire procedure at a faculty meeting and provide each teacher with a copy of all of the materials.
- Have the staff strictly follow the scheduling timeline for each grade level or else the parents with several children in different grade levels will not have appointments back to back (instant headache).
- Have each teacher supply the office with a copy of his or her schedule so the secretary can help parents who have lost their appointment time without disturbing class time. This also comes in handy if a teacher is out on a conference day, so that the appointments may be canceled.

Good luck! Don't hesitate to call if something is not clear.

FIGURE 6.4. TO CONGRATULATE

Dear Proud Frank,

Congratulations on having your school chosen as *High School of the Year* for our state. You and your staff deserve every accolade that comes your way. As a fellow principal, I understand the amount of time, dedication, and hard work that precedes an award of this distinction.

One Wednesday, at your convenience, several of your fellow administrators would like to take you to lunch to salute your accomplishment. Just let me know the best date and the name of your favorite fast food restaurant.

Once again, congratulations. It couldn't have happened to a more deserving person.

Your envious colleague,
Sandy

FIGURE 6.5. TO ANSWER CONCERNS OR CRITICISMS

To: Superintendent Concerned
From: Principal Concerned Also
Re: Eighth Grade State Science Scores

Since you notified me that the Board of Education was

concerned about the drop in the science scores on the state exam in the eighth grade, I have met with the Science Department Head and the entire Science Department. We have had three meetings to develop the following action plan to return the scores to the proper level:

1. A committee of science teachers will meet to compare the material tested on the state exam to our current curriculum.
2. Changes will be made in the curriculum to better reflect the direction of the state exam.
3. Activities at the middle school will not be scheduled at a time that will interfere with the students' total concentration on the exam (i.e., our school concert was scheduled the night before the exam this year).
4. Science teachers will devote more time to thinking and problem-solving skills.
5. Each eighth grade class will set aside review time before the state exam.

Please notify the Board of Education of our action plan to rectify the lowered test scores. I and my staff are also prepared to review our findings with the Board.

FIGURE 6.6. TO SHOW SYMPATHY

Dear Angelo,

I am deeply saddened by the loss of Bob. I know he was a close friend and an important member of your staff. His expertise in the math classroom will be sorely missed by the community and the district.

The staff at Tremont has offered to cover classes at your school so members of the faculty will be able to attend the funeral. We can cover ten classes.

The staff and the PTA have sent a contribution to the Heart Fund in Bob's name. If you need any help during this difficult time, please call on me.

Our thoughts are with you,
Paul

SUMMARY AND TIPS

It's the little things that matter, especially when writing to your peers. The following tips will assist you in all areas of writing but are especially true when communicating with colleagues with whom you wish to maintain an open dialogue:

ON COACHING AND SUPPORTING PEERS

- Give positive recognition immediately.
- Focus your comments on specific behavior.
- Be alert to articles and resources helpful to peers.
- Initiate sharing of written documents and instructional materials.

ON COMMUNICATION EXCHANGES

- Eliminate jargon and educationese.
- Keep it brief and concise.
- Don't talk down, especially to the new kid on the block.
- Use proper grammar and punctuation.
- Be empathetic.
- Be personable. Think of the person as you write.
- Use strong and active verbs.
- Remember organizational skills. The five W's and H is a good old standby.
- Use a summary ending for a quick second reading.
- Using uppercase letters in e-mail is the same as shouting at someone in conversation.
- Using e-mail is not an excuse for spelling and grammar errors.
- Don't write when you are angry unless the message is destroyed and rewritten at a calmer time.
- Be careful with the use of cc. Also, do not forward a peer's writing to another person without permission.
- Read the communication out loud, before sending. Place yourself in the receiver's shoes.

RESOURCES

BOOKS AND ARTICLES

Title: *Motivating Others: Creating the Conditions*
Author: David P. Thompson
Publisher: Eye On Education, 1996

The author places an emphasis on "creating the conditions" for principals to provide feedback, coaching, and guidance to staff. He takes what is known about building teacher motivation and applies this knowledge to principals' work.

WORKSHOPS AND SEMINARS

The workshops and seminars listed in this guide were chosen for their appeal to school administrators. Since the publication of this text, some seminars may have been upgraded or replaced and others may no longer be offered. Similarly, costs and locations may have also changed. We recommend that you contact the consulting group directly for current information and availability.

Title: *Managing for Commitment*
Consulting Group: Center for Creative Leadership
Contact Number: Tel: 919-277-7210

Effective management requires working with people. This seminar focuses on three critical areas: evaluating interpersonal effectiveness, creating a climate of commitment, and developing the potential of others.

Title: *Coaching and Mentoring*
Consulting Group: National Association of Secondary School Principals
Contact Number: Tel: 703-860-0200

A developmental workshop for school administrators designed to build coaching and mentoring skills. Program format is built around small group simulations with lots of practice and feedback from trainers and participants.

Title: *Leader 123*
Consulting Group: National Association of Secondary School Principals
Contact Number: Tel: 703-860-0200

Developmental workshop designed to aid principals and other administrative personnel in the improvement of instructional leadership skills. Participants are required to develop and present a written proposal on an upcoming instructional change they would like to implement in their school.

7

WRITING TO YOUR LOCAL COMMUNITY

"When people communicate,
there are no limits to what they can do."
—Anonymous

YOUR PUBLIC RELATIONS CHALLENGE

Jack McCall (1994) in his text, *The Principal's Edge*, asserts that "effective schools are run by principals, teachers, parents, students, and other stakeholders who know why the school exists" (p. 22). Part of building and strengthening trust and open lines of communication is to involve all the stakeholders. A dynamic school leader involves everyone in the process of developing a productive school. In these learning communities people work hard, show enthusiasm, and expend lots of energy. "They are people who have been inspired to want to work hard for something they really believe in" (p. 23).

Principals generally do a good job keeping staff, parents, teachers, and students informed about the school. However, most principals tend to neglect members of their local community, the other stakeholders (Podsen, 1987). Drake and Roe (1994) support this idea and suggest a possible reason:

> Schools in general have not kept pace with the means and desire for the interconnected operation becoming more prevalent in our economic and to a lesser degree political environment. Is the resistance to interacting with the community at large and parents in particular based on the need to control the educational enterprise? (p. 53)

These other stakeholders include powerful individuals who "influence the directions and actions of various community organizations" (Pawlas, 1995, p. 74). Behind the political scenes these other stakeholders are business leaders, store managers, real estate agents, local and state legislators, bank presidents, school board members, church leaders, store clerks, and community agency employees. All of these citizens come into contact with large numbers of local people and they can have a serious impact on the operation of schools.

Exercise 7.1
Who's in Charge

Let's examine the issue raised by Drake and Roe. Do you feel "outside" involvement of parents and community members is an intrusion on your legitimate authority? What influence have political figures, business leaders, and parents made on schooling in your local community...the national community? What does joint ownership in the educational process mean to you? Remember what we said earlier. It's time to take a fresh look at business as usual.

It Pays to Advertise

Do you know who the key opinion leaders are in your local community? More important, do you have a plan to network with these individuals? What about senior citizen groups (our rising majority of Baby Boomers) non-parents, and parents of students attending private and parochial schools? All these citizens pay taxes and vote on issues that affect schools. They need to know their contributions are paying off.

How involved are these citizens in your school? Recent emphasis on the importance of parental knowledge and involvement in the life of public schools has been growing; however, this same emphasis needs to be applied to general community members. Furthermore, we do know that PR-101 is not included in many administrative preparation programs. Pubic relations strategies and the types of writing targeted for general audiences may be discussed but application and practice is rarely included.

TAPPING INTO YOUR LOCAL COMMUNITY

This audience is no longer the quiet majority. Principals need to develop communication channels that not only inform but also sway this increasingly influential source of support or negative press. How does this happen? What can principals do? Here's a start:

- **Do a Reality Check.** When was the last time you surveyed your local community (not just parents) to find out what they thought about your school? Principals need to be effective problem solvers but current information is critical to the decision-making process. To get this information you will need to demonstrate the ability to plan and write surveys and questionnaires. The companion workbook to this text (*Attacking Your In-Basket: The Principal's Guide to Better Job Writing*) offers several samples.
- **Create a School with a Unifying Purpose.** Why does your school exist? What is unique or special about your school, staff, students, or curriculum programs? Tons of stuff have been written about effective leadership. What's your vision, dream, idea? Have you shared this vision with your school audiences, including the local community? That is to say: Have you advertised what you're doing through brochures, bulletins, flyers, packets targeted for general audiences?
- **Involve the Other Stakeholders.** Collaboration and team building means including all the stakeholders in the process of designing successful and productive schools. The challenge in our largely bureaucratic way of doing business is to create special ways to help individual schools keep parents and citizens intimately associated and involved with the schools. We know schools play an important role in the political and economic functioning of local communities; schools with strong educational programs, competent teachers, and productive students attract businesses and residents. Participatory management is the call of the '90s. Are you still operating in the '80s?

- **Initiate Open Lines of Communication.** The principal's public relations challenge is to assert the credibility of the school. Communicating with teachers and parents may not be enough for schools to survive turbulent political forces seeking to undermine their existence. Regular and systematic lines of communication need to be established with the local community. While your school district does this at a county level, principals need to do this within the local level. Pawlas (1995) suggests these methods:
  - Identify key communicators who can influence and spread accurate information between the school and the local community. Rumors and negative press can be halted when hit head on!
  - Publish a monthly PR Letter highlighting key issues and school achievements. Send a copy to your list of ***Very Important People*** in the community.
  - Hold quarterly meetings with key communicators to provide hands-on demonstrations of school programs and facilities.
  - Sponsor adult education programs aimed at nonparent citizens.
  - Keep your finger on the pulse of the community through special school day programs for grandparents, career exploration, community leaders, and retired school employees.
  - Broadcast school programs and accomplishments through public service announcements.
  - Write news releases and stories to announce events and activities open to the public.
  - Display a message board outside the school publicizing staff and students.

Exercise 7.2
What Do Your Community Members Want to Know?

Identify a group of key communicators from your local community. Find out what they want to know about schools in general, and about your school specifically. Seek out the communication channels and methods that would work best in your setting. Don't forget, your computer can play an important role in this networking process! Do you have a web page?

THE PRINCIPAL REPORTER

So far we have discussed what you can do internally to connect with your local community. But another channel exists that makes us very uncomfortable, the news media. As a principal have you relied on your central office staff to deal with the media? What is your role in publicizing school activities? Pawlas (1995) points out that it's the principal's job to "tell the school's story to the community"; however, he states that "many school administrators put a low priority on media relations" (p. 107).

Pawlas emphasizes the importance of keeping the media and the general community well informed about "what is going on in the school, who is doing it, and why the stories are being made" (p. 108). It doesn't take a rocket scientist to figure out that the media is a major communication channel to the community. Principals need to make it a practice to keep local newspapers, radio, and television channels informed. Here are ten media rules:

1. Get to know your local news reporters on a first name basis.
2. Find out what the media wants to know and when they need to get it.
3. Return phone calls to reporters ASAP.
4. Protect your credibility. Be sincere, honest, and direct.
5. Show your appreciation for good media coverage.
6. Check your facts, dates, and names.
7. Don't send in stories dealing with past events.
8. Don't avoid dealing with the media. Playing hide and seek is a dangerous game.
9. Don't gloss over a problem or situation.
10. Carefully edit all news releases and articles for errors and tone.

NEWS RELEASES AND STORIES

Answering the question, "What does my school community want to know about my school, staff, and students?" should generate ideas for newsworthy press releases and human interest stories. In addition, reviewing upcoming school events and activities on a monthly basis may also target subjects of possible interest to your local news reporters. Remember the media is looking for a new twist on an idea or event. Events that happen in all schools must have an unusual or interesting appeal to attract media coverage. This might include a successful new program, a student who has distinguished himself or herself, or the presence of a celebrity in your midst. The following is an example of a press release.

FIGURE 7.1. PRESS RELEASE

MABRY MIDDLE SCHOOL
Beth Thompson, Press contact
Tel: 778-345-7878

JAZZ TEAM CATCHES THE BEAT

Sixth, seventh, and eighth graders from Mabry Middle School will help bring holiday cheer for local senior citizens with a dance exhibition scheduled for 2:00 p.m. Friday, December 15, at the Twin Towers Community Center.

The jazz fest will feature holiday songs and dances from around the world. Jane Ryan, a leg amputee, will perform a special solo number.

The dance exhibition is free and open to the public. The students will serve refreshments after the performance.

We know too often the media is attracted to the "outrageous" or "far-out." This fascination for sensational and often negative news must be balanced with reporting the more typical and positive school events and activities. Principals must work at combating this trend by taking an active public relations role.

Exercise 7.3
WRITING FOR THE MEDIA

Identify at least ten story ideas about your school. Using the Five W's and H (who, what, where, why, and how) develop at least one press release on an upcoming event in your school. Then write a short news article describing this event. Refer to the companion guide for more writing tips on news releases and news stories.

SUMMARY

To make sure that your local community is given the positive aspects of your school, you will need to reassess how you communicate with important opinion leaders in your community and how you involve all stakeholders in the business of running your school. Today's citizens are better educated, more inquisitive about school operations, more demanding for their children's educational experiences, and more critical of school leaders than ever before. Putting our head in the sand will not change these trends. Principals may need to take the bull by the horns or risk being gored in this public arena.

RESOURCES

BOOKS AND ARTICLES

Title: *The Administrator's Guide to School-Community Relations*
Author: George Pawlas
Publisher: Eye On Education, 1995

This sourcebook contains practical ideas and samples for building parent and family involvement in the school, using the news media to your advantage, planning for crisis situations, preparing job writing documents, and working with local businesses and other stakeholders.

Title: *Bridging Differences: Effective Intergroup Communication*
Author: William Gudykunst
Publisher: Sage Publications, 1991

Working with community groups means dealing with people from different cultural and ethnic backgrounds. The author offers suggestions to managers in assessing stereotypes and making sure we don't misinterpret messages received from various groups

SEMINARS AND WORKSHOPS

The workshops and seminars listed in this guide were chosen for their appeal to school administrators. Since the publication of this text, some seminars may have been upgraded or replaced and others may no longer be offered. Similarly, costs and locations may have also changed. We recommend that you contact the consulting group directly for current information and availability.

Title: *The New Principal, Politics, and the Community*
Consulting Group: National Association of Secondary School Principals
Contact Number: Tel: 703-860-0200

This seminar empowers principals to do more with less. Topics include becoming more receptive to change, more community-oriented, and more politically focused on issues and processes impacting schools.

Title: *Partnerships*
Consulting Group: National Association of Secondary School Principals
Contact Number: 1-800-253-7746

No one person can set a vision for a school. Good working relationships are needed with staff, but also with parents, community leaders and groups, social service agencies, and government organizations. This program helps principals to develop practical approaches to building effective partnerships in their own work environment.

CHAPTER REFERENCES

Drake, T., & Roe, W. (1994). *The principalship*. New York: Macmillan.

Elam, S. (Ed.). (1993) *The state of the nation's public schools: A conference report*. Bloomington, IN: Phi Delta Kappa.

McCall, J. (1994). *The principal's edge*. Princeton, NJ: Eye On Education.

National School Public Relations Association. (1981). Involvement is key to support or commitment. *Principal's Survival Kit.* Arlington, VA: NSPRA.

Ordovensky, P., and Marx, G. (1993). *Working with the news media.* Arlington, VA: American Association of School Administrators.

Pawlas, G. (1995). *The administrator's guide to school community relations.* Princeton, NJ: Eye On Education.

Podsen, I. (1987) *School administrators: The role of writing apprehension on job related writing tasks and writing proficiency*. Unpublished Dissertation. Atlanta, GA: Georgia State University.

8

Writing to Your Professional Community

"Find a subject you care about and which you in your heart feel others should care about. It is the genuine caring, and not your games with language, which will be the most compelling elements in your style."

—Kurt Vonnegut

Writing for educational journals probably isn't very high on your list of things to do. Yet, for those who have tried their hand at this important and gratifying means of communication, there is great reward. As a principal, you have valuable experience and information to share. Whether the topic is about a successful pilot program or simply an opportunity to create good will, the principal who writes for publication shares his or her professional stories and ideas.

Kenneth Henson (1991) talks about six myths or false ideas that plague most writers and especially block the efforts of beginners. He lists these false ideas as:

1. I'm not sure I have what it takes.
2. I don't have the time to write.
3. I don't have anything worth writing about.
4. The editors will reject my manuscript because my name isn't familiar to them.
5. My vocabulary and writing skills are too limited.
6. There are few opportunities to publish in my field. (pp. 24-25)

Think about some of the more important lessons you have learned as a principal. Do those lessons deserve to be shared? We think so. Unfortunately, may of us falsely believe there isn't a market for these lessons or that we don't have a message meriting a "scholarly treatment." Our purpose in this chapter is to convince you that you can and should write for educational journals—to share with others the craft knowledge you have at your fingertips.

TARGETING YOUR MESSAGE

Selecting what you want to write about and how to present your message is entirely up to you. Unlike our university colleagues, we don't need to consider whether a journal is refereed or not. That's not to say writing for one of these journals is out of the question. However, you do have greater latitude in determining the message and targeting the audience. Consider some of the following topics and the audience that might be attracted to them:

TOPIC	AUDIENCE
School-Wide Discipline Plans	Principals-Superintendents-School Boards Teachers
School-Community Relations	Principals-Superintendents-Public Relations Staff
Innovative Programs	Principals-Teachers-Curriculum Supervisors-Parents
Stress and Conflict Management	Principals-Teachers-Counselors-Personnel Managers
Craft Knowledge and Practice	Principals-Superintendents-Teachers

Add additional topics and suggested audiences to this matrix. You may be surprised at the number of topics you can write about.

Our point is to illustrate two things: You have a lot to write about and there is an audience for the message you desire to communicate. The key for novice journal writers is to WRITE. As Henson (1995) so clearly states: "Getting something on paper is half the challenge. You can do it. Just write " (p. 44).

WRITING CAN BE EASY

The quickest way to get your ideas on paper is to "let go." Put your ideas down by creating a mindmap. Let's try one.

- Draw a circle or square in the center of a page.
- Jot down a key word or phrase.
- Start drawing branches and other circles as you brainstorm ideas.
- Use colored pens to group related ideas or topics.
- Add subsets to your ideas.
- Keep going until you run out of ideas.
- Do not edit.
- Review your mindmap for key points and details.

Exercise 8.1
CREATING A MINDMAP

Think about a topic for a professional journal that you would like to write about. Using the mindmap outline below start to generate your thoughts. Keep adding branches and circles until you run out of ideas.

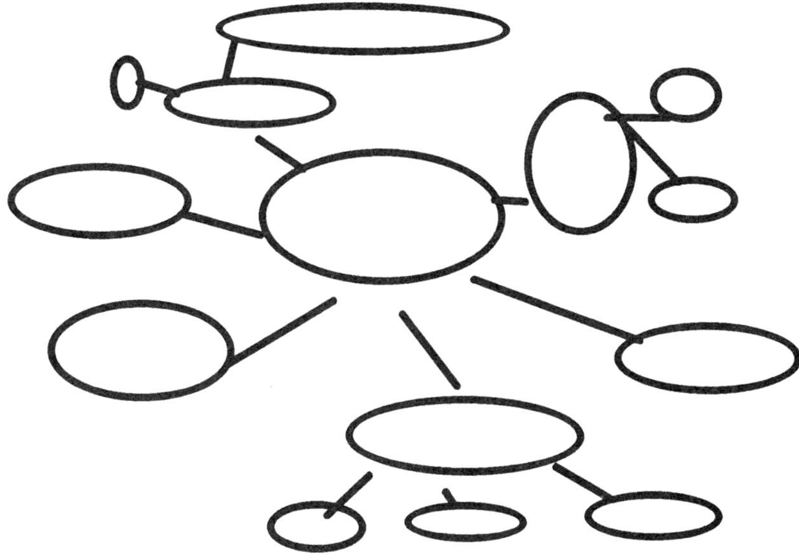

When you mindmap you allow your thoughts to leap across the page until you finally arrive at a thought or idea that CLICKS. Mindmapping allows you to tap into your subconscious mind. You don't have to worry about sentences or correct writing. Joyce Wycoff (1991) states it this way:

> The only thing we have to offer in our writing is the sum of our individual experiences filtered through our singular combination of talents, perspective and consciousness. When we allow the truth of our individuality to emerge in our writing, we are expressing our creativity. When we can express our individuality so that it touches a responsive chord in others, we have reached creative communication (p. 62).

Now you have created a brainstorming web of your ideas on a certain topic. Where do you go from here? Look carefully at your web. Do you see a theme emerging? Review the big picture of your interconnected ideas. You have developed a visual blueprint of your ideas and thinking. What important message can be constructed from this design?

USING GRAPHIC ORGANIZERS

Once you have generated your ideas for a topic, the next step is to organize them to suit your purpose. A quick way for you to do this is to use a graphic organizer. Earlier in the guide we outlined ten different ways for you to organize your writing products; here we suggest using visual tools based on the same patterns for organizing information in your journal articles. Here is one you might use for developing a problem-solution framework (Figure 8.1).

Exercise 8.2
CREATING YOUR OWN VISUAL ORGANIZERS

Once you have decided your organizational approach use your computer to design a visual organizer to assist you in focusing your ideas. There are many resources available to you if this strategy appeals to you (Hyerle, 1996). Writing, we know, is no longer considered a linear process. Current learning theory has helped us to see the importance of relationships and nonlinear connections as the source of new knowledge and ideas. One

FIGURE 8.1. GRAPHIC ORGANIZER SAMPLE
ORGANIZATIONAL STRATEGY: PROBLEM/SOLUTION

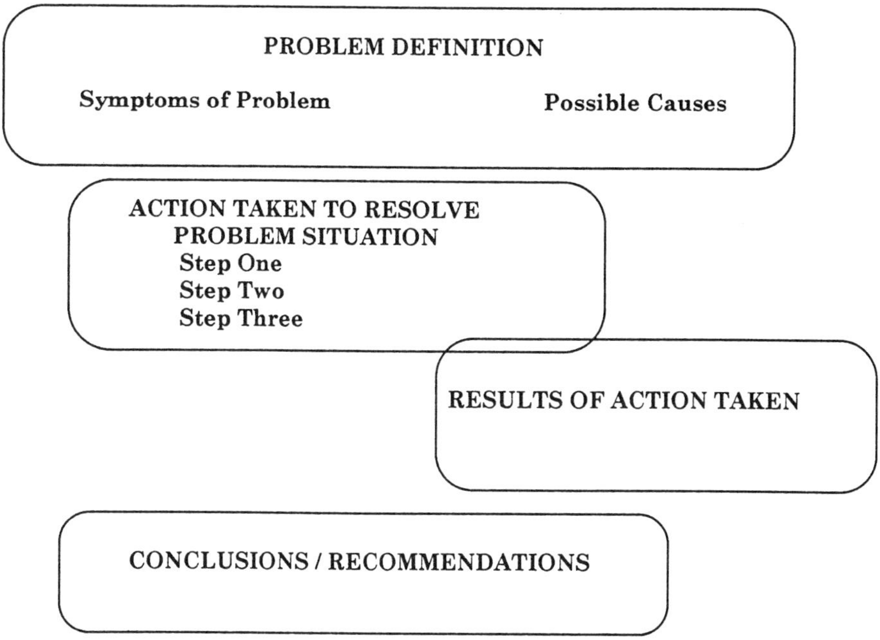

way to do this is to create organizational forms that help this process (Wheatley, 1992).

GET A NEW SLANT

Like good news stories, journal articles should show a novel slant on a situation, an unusual perspective to a problem, or a different angle to a typical school program. Talk to people in your intended audience about the topic. LISTEN to the people directly involved in the situation you want to write about. Add this information to your mindmap or visual organizer. Now you can begin to write your first draft using your mindmap and visual organizer to guide your efforts.

DECISIONS, DECISIONS—JOURNAL A OR JOURNAL B?

Once you have determined your message or topic that others could be interested in, the next step is to find the medium for that message. We're all familiar with journals that target selected audiences as well as some that have a broader focus. Included in the targeted audience category are the *NASSP Bulletin, The American School Board Journal,* and the *Journal of Reading,* just to name a few. Broader focus journals include *Phi Delta Kappa* and *Educational Leadership.*

All of these are nationally known periodicals with a readership ranging from 18,000 to over 150,000. Contrary to what you might believe, the contributors to the three largest periodicals in this group are largely non-university personnel (*Phi Delta Kappa,* June 1993). Information about a journal will help guide you in selecting the right journal for your topic. Reading and studying a journal prior to writing your final draft is critical to your success. Consider these aspects:

- Are the issues "theme" or topical oriented?
- What is the typical content of the journal?
- What is the preferred writing style of the journal?
- What is the acceptance rate for unsolicited material?
- What is the preferred length?
- How many issues are published each year?
- What is the timeline, from submission of an article to the publication date?
- Who makes the final decision about publication?
- How are manuscripts to be submitted? Hard copy, disk or both?

How do you know which journal will publish your work? You don't! However, it only makes sense that a periodical with similar interests and goals as yours is more likely to read your manuscript. Henson (1995) advises, "Choose a journal with a readership and publication requirements that match your goals. Read several issues and pay close attention to the style and tone of the articles" (p. 216).

LOOK CLOSE TO HOME

So far we have discussed selecting the right journal, assuming you want to reach a large audience. However, there are numerous other publication opportunities on a local, state, and regional level. Many state professional organizations publish newsletters and monthly bulletins. Seek out these possibilities and get your feet wet!

Practitioners are constantly looking for ways to improve their schools, their students' successes, and themselves. They often find this help through the many local, state, and regional affiliate publications of Phi Delta Kappa (PDK), The Association for Supervision and Curriculum Development (ASCD), and the National Associations of Elementary (NAESP) and Secondary School Principals (NASSP). Editors of these publications actively seek the practitioner's point of view. If you've never written for an educational journal, these publications offer an excellent opportunity to share your "creative communication."

AUDIENCE/TOPIC STRATEGY ANALYSIS

Earlier in this chapter we discussed the importance of targeting your message. A matrix displaying selected topics and likely audiences was also presented. Now consider that same information in expanded form as a guide for identifying publication opportunities (Figure 8.2).

FIGURE 8.2. AUDIENCE/TOPIC STRATEGY ANALYSIS

TOPIC	AUDIENCE
School-Wide Discipline Plans	Principals-Superintendents-School Boards-Teachers **Publication Opportunity**
School-Community Relations	Principals-Superintendents-Pubic Relations Staff **Publication Opportunity**
Innovative Programs	Principals-Teachers-Parents-Curriculum Supervisors **Publication Opportunity**
Stress and Conflict Management	Principals-Teachers-Counselors **Publication Opportunity**
Craft Knowledge and Practice	Principals-Superintendents-Teachers **Publication Opportunity**

Exercise 8.3
PUBLICATION IDEAS AND POSSIBLE JOURNALS

Develop your own list of publication opportunities for the topics listed here and the ones you added. Seek out a colleague who is also interested in writing an article for publication. Share your ideas.

READABILITY, PLEASE

- As we have stated (and probably overstated), throughout this guide, organizing your writing is critical to a successful end product. Select an organizational strategy or a combination of organizing principles to telegraph your message clearly and concisely.
- Use headings and subheadings to alert your reader to what's coming. They should also pack meaning. Remember, almost no one will read everything you have written.
- Visuals sell your message. Who said, "A picture is worth a thousand words?" Graphs and illustrations are important when you are trying to get your ideas across. Here's a suggested format: Major Headings, Visual, Subheadings, Text.
- Revise, Edit, Revise.

SUMMARY

William Wybel, a principal from Maine, captures the spirit of this chapter. In his article, *Reflection Through Writing,* published in *Educational Leadership* (1991) he expresses his ideas about the benefit of joining a writing group. Here is his introduction:

> The year is 1982, and I am sitting through a series of lectures offered through the Principal's Center at Harvard University. Someone mentions that a writing course is being offered. Write?, I think. Write for an audience of other educators? Someone must be kidding! Writing workshops are only for those folks who write poems or short stories, not for a new-to-the-profession short-time principal who just wants to have a place to put pen to paper and record his thoughts about what happens during the long, lonely hours of the job.

> So I wandered about the fringes of the writing group, trying to find out what went on there. After some internal struggle, I admitted that one of the many challenges ahead of me was to learn how to communicate clearly. I signed up for the next year. (p. 45)

RESOURCES

BOOKS AND ARTICLES

Title: *Visual Tools*
Author: David Hyerle
Publisher: Association for Supervision and Curriculum Development, 1996

The author suggests that three types of tools can help writers construct knowledge, organize information, and communicate their learning with others: brainstorming webs, task-specific organizers, and thinking process maps. This book explains what visual tools are, why we should use them, and how to get the most out of these tools.

Title: *How to Get Your Teaching Ideas Published*
Author: Jean Stang
Publisher: Walker and Co., 1994

The author presents a writer's guide to educational publishing.

CHAPTER REFERENCES

Henson, K.T. (1995). *The art of writing for publication.* Needham Heights, MA: Allyn and Bacon.

Henson, K.T. (1991). Six myths that haunt writers. *The Writer 104*: 24-25.

Hyerle, D. (1996). *Visual tools for constructing knowledge.* Alexandria, VA: Association for Supervision and Curriculum Development.

Roddick, E. (1984). *Writing that means business: A manager's guide.* New York: Macmillan.

Strunk, W. Jr., and White, E.B.(1979). *The elements of style* (3rd ed.). New York: Macmillan.

Wheatley, M.J. (1992). *Leadership and the new science.* San Francisco: Berrett-Koehler Publishers, Inc.

Wybel, W. (1991). *Reflections through writing.* Educational Leadership, 48 (6), 45.

Wycoff, J. (1991). *Mindmapping*. New York: Berkley Books.

Zinsser, W. (1985). *On writing well* (3rd ed.). New York: Harper & Row.

Part Three

Communication That Means Business

Inside the Principal's Office

Mr. Bentley, the principal of Anywhere School, has had a terrible day. His morning began with a flat tire just after he left home and he was already running late. Frustration mounted when he got to the school parking lot and found his parking place taken by an unknown car.

That was just the beginning. Things continued downhill: two very irate parents waited to see him as he entered the main office, a dozen urgent phone calls from the central office, the school newsletters late from the printer, and four teachers absent with only three substitutes available.

And on top of this, the superintendent called and wanted a status report on his school improvement goals ASAP for an upcoming board meeting.

Bill Bentley held his breath and began his deep breathing exercises, lowering his blood pressure which he knew was climbing into the red zone. Bill has been here before and knows that "this too shall pass." Meanwhile, in handling the events of the day, his in-basket has been pushed to the side.

Later, with his wife and children watching television and his late dinner downed, Bill sits in his study and stares at the pile of stuff that has accumulated in his in-basket. The task seems endless: every letter and memo is different; each request and complaint wanting an immediate and satisfactory response. Bill's mind goes blank. His analytical skills are short-circuited by the task of simply reading the information, let alone responding. But the bottom line is this: Bill finds writing difficult and time-consuming. He avoids writing whenever given the choice. When the avoidable becomes unavoidable, he's left dealing with his in-basket, at home, ALONE.

Bill has fallen into a pattern that is repeated each day by many school administrators who just don't like to write. Without being aware of it, and faced with multiple writing tasks simultaneously, the reluctant writer keeps putting off writing tasks, especially the more difficult ones, until the last minute. Then when there is no time left to plan the writing task, the reluctant writer responds. The product, however, often results in a message that is irrelevant and poorly organized.

Ten areas that school administrators identify as problem areas in their writing are:

1. Conciseness
2. Clarity of meaning
3. Success in communicating the purpose
4. Spelling
5. Sentence clarity and variation
6. Paragraph organization
7. Document organization
8. Sensitivity to the audience's perspective
9. Awareness of the needs of the reader
10. Awareness of tone.

HOW TO USE PART THREE

The following two chapters have been designed to be used as a way for you to develop your game plan in attacking your writing tasks. Their purpose is threefold:

- to help you reassess what you need to know about effective writing;
- to review the three types of writing principals use most often on the job; and
- to assist you in developing writing strategies that will help you in writing these products faster and with confidence.

The companion guide to this text, *Disk with Workbook to Accompany Written Expression: The Principal's Survival Guide,* extends the information in these chapters by including competency training modules on each of the writing types principals encounter on the job. Each module presents all or a combination of the following elements:

- key information on the writing form,
- before and after samples to review,
- document analyses to highlight effective writing strategies,
- practice exercises to reinforce effective writing behaviors, and
- document templates (in hard copy and on disk) to get you started faster.

The workbook contains eight training modules:

Memos
Business Letters
Reports
School Forms, Notes, Awards, and Bumper Stickers
Newsletters, News Articles, and Press Releases
Brochures, Bulletins, Flyers, and Posters
Surveys and Questionnaires
Career Résumés

9

Sharpening Your Writing Skills

"With sixty staring me in the face, I have developed inflammation of the sentence structure and definite hardening of the paragraph."
—James Thurber

Effective writing skills form the foundation for successful written communication. They are so basic that quite often we forget their significance or assume we are skillful. We EMPHASIZED in Part One of this guide that the ultimate purpose of your written communication is to build trust and solid working relationships within your school community. To do this you must establish your ability to communicate your ideas clearly and successfully. This chapter presents information in five areas to help you master these skills.

Writing Clearly and Concisely

When asked, "What bugs you about your writing or the writing of other principals?" the majority of administrators describe their writing as "too long," or "it lacks clarity." This aspect is a major problem for most adult writers. If this is a problem area for you, use the following checklist to help you achieve more clarity and conciseness in your writing. Remember: *Failing to plan is planning to fail.*

- **Identify your purpose.** Why are you writing; what do you want to accomplish?
- **Think about your audience.** If you are writing to many, picture one person in that audience and write

to that individual. Assess attitude and the amount of information needed.

- **List the key points and ideas you want to address.** Then highlight the points that support your purpose and meet the needs of your audience.
- **Write a first draft.** Next review it for explicitness and brevity. Check sentence length and paragraph construction. Sentences should run between 18-22 words; paragraphs should include three to five sentences on a single topic.
- **Read the document out loud.** What image do you want to project? What tone do you want to convey—helpful, apologetic, objective, caring, appreciative, formal, informal, humorous?
- **Get feedback from a trusted colleague on your writing.** Ask him or her specifically, "What is the message? What is the tone? What is not clear?" When your colleague's understanding of your ideas matches your purpose, then you will know that your purpose in writing is becoming clear.

Exercise 9.1
WRITING CLEARLY AND CONCISELY

Locate several memos or letters. Review those written products that are longer than one page. Rewrite one of these documents following the suggestions outlined above. Compare your BEFORE and AFTER writing samples. Did the recommendations help you to write faster? Is your writing more concise?

WRITING CORRECTLY: GRAMMAR, SPELLING, PUNCTUATION

Principals can't afford to let poor writing get past the school door. It will seriously impact on our professional credibility and the credibility of our school. Our school audiences expect, even demand, that we show a high degree of skill in the technical components of our language. If you are concerned about the basic elements of writing consider the following steps:

1. Ask your secretary to compile a list of your most common

writing errors that he or she finds in your writing.
2. Find a grammar book that you can use as a reference tool in working on your precision in this area. Flag those sections that address your problem areas.
3. If you use a computer (and we think you should) obtain spell checking and grammar checking software programs to use with your writing. A good program can also teach you the rules you are breaking as it checks your work. However, don't assume these programs will catch everything.
4. Create an editing team to proofread all writing that leaves the school.
5. Model the way. Ask teachers to review your writing and encourage them to critique each other's writing. As the instructional leader you should be reviewing formal teacher letters to parents on a regular basis.

USING EDUCATIONAL JARGON

Like most professionals in a specialized career, we develop buzzwords and complex terminology unique to our working world. Memos and letters containing these terms may seem very clear to those within our organization, but they are likely to confuse and frustrate individuals outside our school system.

When writing to a diverse group of individuals such as parents, keep the educationese to a minimum. Better yet, eliminate it. Use the following suggestions to help you determine the effective use of jargon.

- Analyze your audience. If you are writing to staff, the use of common jargon may be appropriate, even desirable. However, parents and professionals outside our school are more likely to be confused or misinterpret these words.
- If the term is unavoidable in a document define the term or use the term in a context that clarifies the meaning.

ELIMINATING UNNECESSARY DETAIL

Part of the problem in writing clearly and concisely is knowing what information is essential and what information can be eliminated or packaged differently. If you follow the steps outlined in the section on *Writing Clearly and Concisely*, you will at least begin the process more efficiently. To help reduce eye strain and extraneous detail, try these suggestions.

- Before tackling a memo or report that includes a large amount of information, list the points or major recommendations you want to make. Summarize this information and then provide the supporting details in an addendum.
- When writing longer documents such as school improvement reports, ask the recipient of the document what information is critical and what can be eliminated.
- Organize the document with clear headings and subheadings. See if you can cover the content using less words.

WRITING WITH PIZZAZZ

Perhaps you feel pretty comfortable with your writing skill. None of these areas are troublesome for you. Then you might be ready to develop a style that's expressive and uniquely your own. This is the touch that compels your reader to keep reading. Consider these guidelines in developing a more interesting writing style.

- Avoid opening your sentences with overused phrases like "It is" and "There are" and "Thank you for your letter on" or " Per your request, please find the enclosed report on ...." Yawn. Z...z...z...z... Grab attention quickly.
- Increase your vocabulary. Look for interesting and dynamic words in your personal and professional reading. Jot them down and check out their meaning. Try to use them in your writing when appropriate. Effective writers select words carefully to carry precise meaning and intended impressions.
- Give your sentences more punch. Use the active voice whenever possible. Use results-oriented action words such as calculated, leveraged, restored, networked, formulated, detected, strategized, etc. For example:

PASSIVE VOICE
Principals are energized by an enthusiastic staff.

ACTIVE VOICE
An enthusiastic staff energizes principals.

The active verb "energizes" is stronger than the passive verb "are energized by." Sentences that reflect the active voice are usually shorter.

- Create visuals to help you illustrate a point and add impact to your writing documents. Computer technology gives us the power of the graphic designer at the touch of the mouse.

Exercise 9.2
YOUR EDITING CHECKLIST

This checklist may provide a strategy to use in checking the basic features of your writing. Select one or two of your writing products and use this checklist to assess your writing.

Organization

I have identified my purpose.
I have assessed my audience.
I have stated my main points clearly.
I have enough details to support my purpose.
I have organized the content logically/sequentially.
I have used effective transitions.

Sentence Structure

My sentence length is between 18 and 20 words.
I have used the active voice.
I have no sentence fragments or run-ons.
My paragraphs include a variety of sentence types.
(Simple, compound, and complex)
The sentences have clear subjects and verbs.

Grammatical Errors

The verbs agree with their subjects.
The pronouns have clear antecedents.
I have not used an adjective in place of an adverb.
None of my modifiers are misplaced.
I have made no shifts in tense.

Word Choice

I have used action-oriented verbs.
I have avoided words with negative connotations.
I have omitted unnecessary words and expressions.
I have avoided clichés and educational jargon.
I have chosen words that say exactly what I mean.
My sentences do not begin with overused phrases.
My writing conveys my intended tone.

Mechanics

No words are misspelled.
I have eliminated unnecessary commas.
I have not used unnecessary quotation marks or exclamation points.
I have made any abbreviations clear.
I have not accidentally omitted a word or sentence.
My document looks professional.
I have used headings and subheadings.
I have varied the font style and size.
I have utilized the computer to enhance my written documents.

SUMMARY AND TIPS

"People forget how fast you did a job—
but they remember how well you did it."
—NASSP Great Quotations

Remember these three writing principles offered by Joyce Wycoff (1991):

> First and foremost: No one wants to read it!
>
> Second and important: Almost no one will read all of it!
>
> Third and critical: Almost everyone will misunderstand some part of it (p. 69). Therefore,

- Keep sentences and paragraphs short.
- Write like you speak to make your writing more readable.
- Plan your written documents before beginning to write.
- Consider your audience and their needs.

- Edit and proofread all your correspondence for common errors.
- Use a variety of sentence openers and sentence structures.
- Eliminate the use of jargon.
- Increase your vocabulary.
- Use charts, tables and graphics to reinforce your message.
- Allocate time for writing.
- Seek feedback on your writing.

RESOURCES

BOOKS AND ARTICLES

Title: *The Elements of Style*
Author: W. Strunk and E.B. White
Publisher: Macmillan, 1979

A well known reference on grammar and style emphasizing conciseness and clarity. The authors select common writing problems and offer practical writing suggestions.

Title: *The Little English Handbook: Choices and Conventions*
Author: Edward Corbett
Publisher: Scott, Foresman, and Co., 1987

Highlights 50 areas of grammar, style, and sentence mechanics that trouble adult writers.

SEMINARS AND WORKSHOPS

The workshops and seminars listed in this guide were chosen for their appeal to school administrators. Since the publication of this text, some seminars may have been upgraded or replaced and others may no longer be offered. Similarly, costs and locations may have also changed. We recommend that you contact the consulting group directly for current information and availability.

Title: *Writing, Speaking, and Listening for Successful Communication*
Consulting Group: American Management Association
Contact Number: Tel: 518-891-0065

A communication seminar for managers that deals with situation and audience analysis, determining proper communication channels, and writing concise, understandable messages.

Title *Writing with Impact*
Title: *From the Desk of… A Written Communication Program for School Administrators*
Consulting Group: National Association of Secondary School Principals
Contact Number: Tel: 703-860-0200

Developmental programs that engage participants in multiple writing tasks based on the job demands in the principalship. The programs help principals to reflect on writing behaviors, practice effective writing, and give and receive feedback on documents produced on the job.

COMPUTER SOFTWARE

Title: *Grammatik 5*
Vendor: Word Perfect Corp.
Contact Number: Tel: 800-321-4566

Title: *Right Writer*
Vendor: Que Software
Contact Number: Tel: 800-992-0244
Provides grammar and style checkers for editing your writing.

CHAPTER REFERENCES

Wycoff, J. (1991). *Mindmapping*. New York: Berkley Books.

10

Attacking Your In-Basket: Writing Better Memos, Letters, and Reports

"People seldom improve when they have no other model but themselves to copy after."
—Goldsmith
NASSP Great Quotations

During the course of the day, administrators grapple with a multitude of writing tasks from short memos to lengthy school improvement reports. Each type of writing requires a specific approach in order to be effective. Our purpose in this chapter is to highlight the *Do's and Don'ts* about the writing types principals use most often on the job: memos, letters, and short reports.

Before you begin to write, you may find it helpful to review sample memos and letters similar to the ones you need to write on the job. These exhibits are writing documents from our colleagues in various school locations. Exposure to examples of best practice enables you to adapt these writing products to meet your writing style, purpose, and audience. The companion guide to this text (*Attacking Your In-Basket: The Principal's Guide to Better Job Writing*) presents additional writing types principals use on the job. We show each type with *Do's and Don'ts* and examples for you to review. Also, we accompany each sample with a *Document Analysis* to help target the effective writing behaviors demonstrated by the writer.

However, before attacking those items found in every principal's in-basket, we thought a brief summary of the writing dimensions covered in this guide would be helpful.

CRITICAL WRITING DIMENSIONS

Throughout various chapters of this guide, we have centered your attention on four critical writing dimensions:

- **Your PURPOSE for writing.**
  What do you want to happen?
- **Your AUDIENCE:**
  Staff, parents, central office, peers, students, community
- **Your ORGANIZATIONAL strategy**
  Chronological Order, Topic Order, Need/Plan/Benefit, Problem/Solution, Question/Answer, etc.
- **Your TONE**
  Collaborative, Authoritative, Complimentary, Objective, Friendly, Supportive

In addition to these four aspects we want to center your attention on **FORM**. Purpose and form deal with a wide range of possibilities available to you. The following table shows you how purpose and form are closely linked and provides you with a useful framework in developing any written communication document. Such a framework, when considered with an organizational strategy, your intended audience, and tone, should help you in creating effective written products.

FIGURE 10.1. WRITING FORMS

To Inform or Advise

Memos	Minutes of meetings
Business letters	Invitations
Newsletters	Programs
Brochures	E-mail
Flyers	Reports
Forms	Agendas
Posters	School calendars
Brochures	Speeches
School handbooks	

To Command or Direct

Memos/Letters requiring specific action	School Rules and Regulations for safety and health
Instructions	Letters of reprimand
Directions	E-mail
Policy and Procedures	

To Describe

Anecdotal records	Parent-Teacher conference guide
Teacher observation notes and scripts	Curriculum guides
Reports of a sequence of events	School newsletters
Professional development plans	News releases
Brochures on school programs	Articles for professional journals
Flyers	Articles for school newsletters

To Persuade

Letters of recommendation	Speeches
Editorials	Applications
Grant proposals	Resumes
Letters/Memos of request	Cover letters
Notes for a debate/meeting	

To Show Appreciation

Letters/Memos of commendation	Special occasion cards
Thank you notes	Staff-student-parent recognition awards

To Clarify Thinking

Note-taking	Mindmapping
Explanations	Outlines
Jottings of sensory impressions from observations, meetings, conferences	Visual/graphic organizers
Journals	

To Explore and Build Relationships

Questionnaires	Memos/Letters responding to problems/concerns/criticisms
Surveys	School-community public relations plans
Greeting cards	

To Make Comparisons

Charts	Descriptions
Tables	School Improvement Reports
Diagrams, graphs	Program Evaluation Reports

To Predict or Hypothesize

Speculations about probable outcomes in conclusions, recommendations, and development plans	Questions for meetings, conferences, interviews
Professional articles	Proposals

MEMOS MAKE IT HAPPEN

Principals communicate in writing most often to internal audiences such as staff and central office personnel; therefore, memos and letters are the most utilized forms of written communication. Communication by memorandum saves valuable managerial time. The effective administrator knows when and how to use this communication tool to simplify correspondence procedures and to expedite the flow of information between and among members of the school system.

DATE: September 20, 199_
TO: Our Colleagues in the Trenches
FROM: The Authors
SUBJECT: Memo Writing Tips

- "**Memos are a quick call to action.** Be sure the reader understands what you want and when you want it. " As the memo writer, you may need to give information concerning new policies and staff decisions, relay asked-for information, present facts for decision-making by others, report progress on school projects, suggest ideas, justify or set responsibility for certain courses of action, or take a stand on an issue. Memos are useful in making sure that information communicated verbally is not forgotten or misunderstood.
- "**Memos can go up, down, or across the organizational structure.** It's all right to send a memo to the boss." Memos are internal business communications.

The effective principal keeps the superintendent informed and up-to-date on pertinent issues. More important, the effective school leader knows that internal communication cannot be left to chance. Both upward and downward communication channels must be planned and utilized. Generally, you use letters when writing to people outside the organization.

- **A memo is an effective way to express appreciation and build morale within the school.** A short memo to a teacher who has performed an outstanding lesson often has a greater effect than a verbal compliment. Memos acknowledging how staff members have contributed to the school's functioning not only benefits working relationships but also shows that you, as the school leader, have one of the qualities of an effective administrator, the ability to recognize superior performance.
- **The most important part of the memo is the body.** Memos emphasize the important facts, avoiding needless and trivial details. Get to the point quickly by using short words, sentences, paragraphs and listings to keep the reader's interest.
- **Effective memo writers include at least three parts:**

  Introduction: State the purpose of the memo and the method used to obtain information presented.

  Body: Assert the message objectively and include sufficient detailed information. Avoid mixing opinion with facts in this part of the memo.

  Conclusion: Summarize the facts, outline a plan of action or make recommendations for future action. "Personal comments and opinions may be included in this section; however, conclusions must be supported by facts or other evidence presented in the memo" (Hennington, p. 86).
- **Effective memo writers choose an organizational strategy that best suits their purpose.** No rigid rules govern the content and organization of memos. In Figure 10.2 you will see the most frequently used organizational patterns found in businesslike writing.

FIGURE 10.2. ORGANIZATIONAL STRATEGY

ORGANIZATIONAL PATTERN	DESCRIPTION
• Analytical Approach	State situation, your analysis, and conclusions.
• Chronological Approach	List the activities by order of time or sequence.
• Deductive Approach	Start with a summary of conclusions or recommendations; then support with facts and findings.
• Inductive Approach	Open with facts and findings; then present conclusions and/or recommendations. This approach is often used in "giving bad news."
• Need/Plan/Benefit	Begin with a description of the current need in your situation, outline a plan to meet the need, and then state the benefits.
• Problem/Solution	Disclose the dilemma; then offer your solution.
• Topic Approach	Identify the key points and then develop each one. Order of topics is by preference.
• Question/Answer	Raise the issue by asking a question; then answer it.

- **"Keep your audience, not the directive or information, in mind."** Before beginning to write a memo, you should complete this sentence:

  I want (WHO) to do (WHAT) because (REASON).

  If you can't complete this sentence you need to REEXAMINE your audience and your purpose for writing this memo.
- **Know the ten parts to an effective memo as shown in Figure 10.3.**
- **"Make it easy for the reader to take action."** Consider adding a contact line: Ex: "Contact: Call Mr. Glenn Jones in Personnel at extension 381."
- **"Add a response line at the end of the memo."** The reader can jot down a reply and return the memo promptly.

FIGURE 10.3. TEN PARTS TO AN EFFECTIVE MEMO

Memorandum Head	The word MEMORANDUM printed in capital letters at top of paper.
To Line:	Identifies the memo recipient.
From Line:	Identifies the writer.
Writer's Initials	Memo writer's initials by the typed name on FROM LINE.
Date Line	For both reference and legal reasons, all memos should be dated.
Subject Line or Action Requested Line	Announces the topic of memo; provides a useful way to file and retrieve correspondence.
Body	Contains the message.
Reference Initials	Reflect the initials of the secretary who prepared the memo.
Enclosure Notation-Enc.,Encl.,Enc.1	Used if one or more items are included with the memo.
Carbon Copy Notation—CC:	Indicates a copy has been directed to another person.

- **Develop a variety of printed memo formats**. Your computer software program usually has formatted templates ready to use.

Adapted from Yerkes, D., and Morgan, S. (1991). *Strategies for Success: An Administrator's Guide to Writing.* Reston, VA: NASSP. pp. 16-17. Direct citations quoted above.

Adapted from Hennington, J. (1978). "Memorandums—An Effective Communication Tool for Managers" in *Business Communication* by Golen, Figgins, and Smeltzer (1984). New York: John Wiley & Sons, pp. 82-89.

FIGURE 10.4. MEMO TO STAFF
PURPOSE: TO PERSUADE
AUDIENCE: TEACHING STAFF
TONE: SUPPORTIVE
STRATEGY: NEED/PLAN/BENEFIT

Document Analysis

TO: Teaching Staff
FROM: E.S. Principal
RE: Teacher Evaluation
DATE: September 12, 199_

The philosophy and purpose of teacher evaluation is to focus our attention on teaching and learning in our school. The process should provide valuable information for us to use in developing the best learning environment for our students; in addition, it should also create a climate that stimulates our own professional growth. The bottom line is, always will be, how staff impacts on our students' well-being and educational progress.

Introduces the topic.

Describes the current need.

One of our district goals developed jointly by the two building teams is to explore alternative assessment methods for both students and teachers. I would like to begin this process with an alternative assessment suggestion for our teacher evaluation program. The Teacher Portfolio Assessment is not a cumbersome process and allows a lot of flexibility in its format and design.

Outlines the plan.

Take some time to review the attached overview of this type of assessment. Think about it, ask questions, and decide if you would like to experiment with it. This is not mandatory; it is strictly voluntary on your part. If you would like to give it a try, work on the goals section and then set up an initial

Provides the supporting details in next paragraph.

meeting with me to begin the process. I would like to have the initial meetings completed by the second week in October. If you decide this assessment process is not for you, you will be evaluated in the same manner used last year.

I hope that many of you will take advantage of this new format. This self-directed goal setting approach to teacher evaluation is fairly new. Research indicates that teachers find it personally rewarding and professionally meaningful. This is something we all hope to find during our careers. Specifically, I believe it will benefit you in three ways:

Summarizes the benefits of plan.

Uses the active voice.

Keeps sentences short and clear.

1. Allows the teacher to identify and set targeted goals based on individual needs, skills, and experiences;
2. Provides flexibility in collecting and reviewing data to support goal achievement;
3. Empowers teachers to take charge of their professional development.

Uses a listing format.

Please let me know your intentions by September 20th so that I can begin my planning and scheduling process.

Indicates action requested.

ES/sf

Reference initials.

Encl.1

Enclosure notation.

FIGURE 10.5. MEMO TO SUPERINTENDENT
PURPOSE: TO INFORM
AUDIENCE: SUPERINTENDENT
TONE: OBJECTIVE
STRATEGY: TOPIC APPROACH

Document Analysis

To: Superintendent
From: H.S. Principal
Re: Quarter Report
Date: December 1, 199_

As we conclude the fall quarter, the status on my 199_ goals is as follows:

States the purpose of the memo.

GOAL #1: To enter Springville High School in the federal High School of Excellence Competition.

Uses bold format to highlight each goal.

Due to an unexpected change by the federal government, the criteria for eligibility for this goal reverted back to the American Disabilities Act of 1970. Therefore, this goal is again viable. The report has been completed and will be mailed by the January 3, 199_ deadline.

Organizes the content by topic.

GOAL #2: To improve the performance of Mr. Johnson.

Observations and professional development plans indicate that Mr. Johnson has incorporated more hands-on materials into his lecture presentations. Through peer observation he is also seeing how a colleague differs in his disciplinary interactions with students. While parent and student complaints are not as frequent, major changes in teaching style and classroom management techniques have not yet been inculcated into Mr. Johnson's instructional delivery. I recommend we continue to monitor his progress through our intensive assistance process.

Sentences are brief and clear. Paragraphs stick to one topic.

GOAL #3: To continue evaluation program for untenured staff.

We are progressing through our six written observations for each staff member as well as our frequent walk-throughs. With the exception of one, our second-year teachers are doing well. Our first-year teachers have varied areas of concern. Mrs. Smith has to raise the level of instructional expectations for both her Law & Marketing students. Ms. Valiant needs to focus on classroom management skills; Mr. Myers is competent but should add more diversity to his instructional delivery. Each of them has been informed of these areas of concern. All untenured staff have also been told that videotaping for the purpose of self-analysis will take place. One teacher has already been taped and reviewed.

Keeps superintendent informed of potential personnel problems.

Documents levels of performance.

HS/gl

Reference initials.

How to Write a Business Letter

Principals write business letters to both internal and external audiences A good business letter can get you help, get you money, or "get you off the hook." According to Malcolm Forbes (*Forbes* Magazine), who has reviewed over 10,000 business letters annually, they fall into three types:

"Stultifying if not stupid
Mundane—most of them
First Rate—most rare" (p. 78)

He offers these suggestions to get the job done RIGHT!

Know What You Want

- Write down your purpose in one sentence.
- List the major points before you write. Answer the 5

W's (Who, What, Where, When, and Why) or develop a mindmap to help organize ideas.

- If responding to a letter, check the points that need attention. Keep it in front of you to avoid omitting a pertinent issue or concern.
- Answer promptly.

JUMP RIGHT IN

- Call the reader by name not "Dear Sir, Madame, or Ms."
- State the purpose in the first paragraph.
- Write the letter from the reader's point of view. Tell what's in it for him or her. Anticipate questions and objections.
- Create a positive impression even if you're delivering bad news. A real PR challenge!
- Write the way you speak. How many times have you started a conversation with "Thank you for your letter dated ...?" Never, we would guess. Be specific, clear, and concise. Keep your letter to one page.
- "Lean heavier on nouns and verbs, lighter on adjectives. Use the active voice instead of passive" (p. 80).

GIVE IT YOUR BEST SHOT

- Use your computer technology to make your letter a real attention getter. Use headings to identify key sections or points. **Experiment with various fonts** to make your letter appealing and easy to read. <u>Underline important words or ideas</u> for emphasis. Failure to produce visually appealing and easy to read documents will put your letter (and your problem) at the bottom of your reader's *To Do List*!
- "Make it perfect. No typos, no misspellings, no factual errors" (p. 80). Remember this message represents you.
- Don't be pretentious, Mr. or Ms. Know It All.
- Don't exaggerate.
- Be honest, direct, and cordial.

- Edit critically. Read your letter out loud.
- Get feedback from a colleague.

SUM IT UP AND GET OUT

- No mystery here. The last paragraph should tell the reader exactly what is expected from him or her or what you're going to do.
- Close and sign legibly.

Adapted from Malcolm Forbes (1981). "How to Write a Business Letter." In *Business Communication* by Golen, Figgins, and Smletzer (1984). New York: John Wiley & Sons, pp. 78-81.

FIGURE 10.6. LETTER OF RECOMMENDATION
PURPOSE: TO RECOMMEND
AUDIENCE: PEER
TONE: COMPLIMENTARY
STRATEGY: INDUCTIVE APPROACH

	Document Analysis
May 9, 199_	
Mr. John Jackson, Principal Fanning City High School 25 Sky Lane Denver, CO 23567	
SUBJECT: Mr. Dan Owen	Subject line.
Mr. Dan Owen has asked me to write a letter of recommendation concerning his application for a teaching position in your school.	First paragraph states the purpose.
Dan Owen was hired in the spring of 1993 as a permanent substitute in social studies for an indefinite period. While we made a commitment to him through the end of June, it was made clear that we didn't know when or if the teacher he was replacing would return. Since the bulk of his teaching schedule terminated in a Global Studies Regents, we were highly concerned about the stu-	Summarizes background information concerning hiring circumstances.

dents' preparation for these difficult exams. As a result of his conscientious efforts and the confidence he inspired in the students, the students completed the year on a very positive note.

Praises teacher and stresses results.

Having observed Mr. Owen in a very difficult set of circumstances and knowing that both students and parents were very pleased with his ability to motivate the reluctant learner, we hired Mr. Owen for a full-time tenured track position when we had the opportunity during the following fall.

Mr. Owen's training and preparation is largely in American History. He has been teaching both Regents and non-Regents eleventh graders over the past two school years. However, wishing to expand his background and make himself more flexible, he requested to teach ninth grade Global Studies on both the Regents and non-Regents level. To his credit, he has expended an inordinate amount of time in order to develop his own expertise in non-Western history. His plans are detailed and include activities that are thought-provoking and require cooperative learning efforts.

Provides specific details regarding teaching background and subjects taught.

Points out teacher's initiative to expand knowledge base.

Dan Owen is an asset to our Social Studies Department and I will regret losing him. He is young and responsive to constructive criticism. He is hard-working and relates to young adults in an extremely positive manner. His classes are interesting and his students truly enjoy them. During his two and a half years, he demonstrated high skill in classroom management. I am sure he will make the same positive contribu-

Ends with strong recommendation.

Summarizes teaching skills and professional qualities.

Sentences are short and clear.

tion to your high school as he has to mine.

Sincerely,

Margaret Mills
Principal

MM/dh

Reference initials

FIGURE 10.7. LETTER TO PARENT
PURPOSE: ALLY A CONCERN
AUDIENCE: PARENT
TONE: OBJECTIVE
STRATEGY: QUESTION/ANSWER

April 15, 199_

Document Analysis

Mrs. Ruth Wilson
2450 Dallis Drive
Annapolis, MD 87690

Dear Mrs. Wilson:

Welcome to Honolulu and the Hawaii District Schools. After our phone conversation on April 13th, I wanted to respond to your questions about discrimination.

States the purpose of the letter. Refers to phone conversation.

Question One: How much discrimination exists between and among the cultures in our school system? In my opinion, discrimination is a relative thing. Most Caucasian children do not experience discrimination from their classmates. Teachers have reported that a few do, but mainly because they themselves do not get along with other children. In recent years, the number of Caucasian children has increased to the point where they are no longer looked upon as different. Further, we are such a melting pot that such differences in culture, race, and

Uses boldface to highlight questions raised by parent and then responds.

The administrator takes an open and tactful approach.

ethnicity are viewed as positive contributions to our school community. School principals and teachers will not tolerate discrimination, and teach toward the acceptance of all cultures and races.

States school position on the issue.

Question Two: Does Hawaii have private schools? Yes, there are several private schools in the local community where you are planning to live. However, I do not recommend sending your children to them unless you hold some strong personal reasons. Attached is the list of private schools you requested.

Responds to parent request.

Enclosed with this letter is a packet of information regarding our school system and the instructional programs available to our parents and students. After reviewing these materials I think you will find our school system equal to the challenge of giving your children a quality educational experience.

Includes information about school for decision making.

I look forward to meeting you and working with your children Should you have further concerns about this issue please contact Jane Smith at 204-555-2323. Jane is a parent in our school system and would be happy to give you her perspective on this issue.

Adds CONTACT reference.

Shows sensitivity to parent viewpoint.

Sincerely,

Kyoto Ambanta
Principal

KA/dh

Encl.2

Adapted from Tomlinson, G. (1984). *School Administrator's Complete Letter Book.* Prentice Hall, p. 219.

SUGGESTIONS FOR BETTER REPORT WRITING

WHY ARE REPORTS TOUGH TO WRITE?

Compared with memos and letters, reports take time to develop. Wakin (1982) states that "they require more data, cover more territory in greater depth, and call for more detailed analysis." In Chapter 1 we point out the benefits of collaborating on school writing projects in order to produce complex writing documents; however, this is a process that takes time and often depends on the writing skills of many committee members.

School administrators are responsible for reporting accurate information on all aspects of the school. You may be asked to submit a short or formal report on a wide range of topics. Keep in mind these critical elements:

WHAT ARE THE BASIC PARTS TO A REPORT?

Reports, whether they are short or long, break down into four basic parts:

SUMMARY
BACKGROUND
BODY
CONCLUSIONS/RECOMMENDATIONS

Writing each section of the report is like writing a paragraph. It requires a grasp of the key points and the ability to organize facts and information. The most important part of any report is the SUMMARY. Usually no longer than one page, the summary tells the reader what you're going to tell him or her. Generally, conclusions and reasons supporting them are the guts of the summary. An effective approach in writing the summary is to use the 5 W's and H:

- **WHO** is reporting—district, school, department, team, individual?
- **WHAT** is the message and what is the evidence supporting the message?
- **WHEN** were the facts and findings gathered, and **HOW** collected?
- **WHERE** did the information search take place?
- **WHY** is this report important and significant?

After reading the summary, the reader should know the key facts in each of these areas. Each section should cover the 5 W's and H in more detail. The body of the report is written first and then the summary. The bottom line in report writing is the same one for all types of writing: *Have you gotten the message across clearly and effectively?* Figure 10.8 shows the components of a formal report.

FIGURE 10.8. WHAT ARE THE COMPONENTS OF A FORMAL REPORT?

• Cover Letter	Prepares the reader by stating purpose and subject of report.
• Report Cover	Contains the title and date. Printed on heavy stock with attractive artwork if appropriate.
• Title Page	Identifies the subject and type of report : Ex: *A Proposal for an After School Tutoring Program.*
• Table of Contents	Reports over four pages with several subsections need a table of contents to help the reader find information without searching through the report. Use the headings and subheadings of your report to develop the table.
• List of Figures and Tables	A list of graphs, charts, tables, and illustrations is placed before the report for easy access by the reader.
• Report Summary	Executive summary or abstract presents the essential information of your report in a concise way. Keep to one page.
• Report Text	The text of the report should include the following parts: *Introduction, Background, Body, Conclusion.*
• Appendixes	Includes material that supports the purpose of the report but is not necessary. Ex: If you used a questionnaire in gathering data, you might want to include a copy of the survey.
• References	Materials used in preparing the report.

WHAT ARE COMMON REPORT WRITING HAZARDS?

Hazard #1: Ignoring Your Audience

Our central theme in this text has concentrated on the importance of audience. Perhaps the gravest error for most administrators is ignoring or not thinking about the needs and attitude of the reader. Reports are usually directed to a specific person or group and have an explicit purpose. One suggestion is to ask the recipient of the report what information is needed and what can be eliminated. The point here is to make sure you have targeted the information required for the reader/committee to make a decision. It beats mindreading and having to go back and redo sections of the report.

Hazard #2: Writing to Impress

Reports need to be understood on the first reading. Nothing turns a reader off faster than writing that is filled with educationese. Reports written with a highbrow impression may also hinder effective communication. Assuming your reader understands your vocabulary and your jargon is a serious ***NO NO***. Your objective is this: *Make sure your reader comprehends your ideas with a minimum of misunderstanding.* Writing to impress is not limited to the use of ambiguous words but also includes nonessential detail and technical trivia. *Remember: short words, short sentences, short paragraphs!*

Hazard #3: Dazzling with Data

A good painter not only knows what to put in a painting, but more importantly, he knows what to leave out. If you dazzle your readers with tons of information, they may be impressed but they may also miss the message. After each section of the report ask yourself these two questions:

- *"What can I remove from this paragraph or section without destroying its meaning and its relationship to what comes before and after?"*
- *"Does my reader require all this data to comprehend, evaluate, or make a decision?"* (Vinci, p. 107)

By reducing excess words, descriptions, and supportive data, you will also reduce eye strain on your readers. In the end you will have a tighter, better, and more readable report.

Hazard #4: Not Accenting

Failure to highlight the "significant elements, findings, illustrations, data, tests, facts, trends, procedures, or results" relative to your subject and purpose of your report will force your reader to do so. Consequently, he or she may consider the report incomplete, draw his or her own conclusions, or hit upon the recommendations by chance. "All the key points of your report should define and focus on the purpose of your report" (Vinci, 107).

Several methods may be used: underlining an important statement or conclusion, pointing out a particular illustration, using a different font size, **bolding a key recommendation,** utilizing headings and subheadings, and developing key sentences in the first or last sentence of a paragraph.

Hazard #5: Omitting Graphics

Here's where your technological expertise is going to pay off! The volume of data available to us as a result of technological advances "often makes it difficult to identify certain trends or patterns." As a school manager and decision maker "you are under a great deal of pressure and time constraints to read, evaluate and interpret data" (Golen & Ellzey, 1984, p. 109).

Did you know that a well-designed graph that fits on one page can summarize pages of written data? "Furthermore, when data are presented graphically, various trends and patterns can be recognized immediately" (p. 109). Failure to utilize this tool may hinder your reader's decision-making time.

Your computer can design and generate tables, charts, graphs, drawings, and diagrams in COLOR. Use of these graphics can provide a powerful tool for management decision making and effective reports.

Adapted from Vinci, V. "Ten Report Writing Pitfalls: How to Avoid Them." In *Business Communication* by Golen, Figgins, and Smeltzer (1984). New York: John Wiley & Sons, pp. 102-108.

Adapted from Wakin, E. (1982). "Better Business Writing." In *Business Communication* by Golen, Figgins, and Smeltzer (1984). New York: John Wiley & Sons, pp. 99-100.

FIGURE 10.9. TEACHING OBSERVATION REPORT
MS. NICKI ANDERSON

PURPOSE: To Describe/To Clarify Thinking
AUDIENCE: Teacher
TONE: Objective
STRATEGY: Inductive Approach and Topic Order

This sample of a short report organizes the content into four parts:

- Overview
- Episode Summary
- Teaching Performance Competencies
- Post-Observation Summary and Reflections

Each part of the report is clearly identified through bold headings and subheadings. The writer describes the classroom observation in an objective, non-judgmental way. The observer uses scripting and anecdotal notes to support conclusions and recommendations. Questions for reflection are raised by the observer in the summary section. The observer intends to use this report as the basis of the post-observation conference with the teacher.

OVERVIEW

On Wednesday, January 31, 199_, I observed Nicki Anderson teaching history to approximately 20 tenth grade students at Amelia Hall High School during second period. The students sat in desks arranged in short vertical rows in a portable trailer. The teacher's desk was located near a side wall by the entrance. A dry erase blackboard and an overhead were positioned at the front of the room.

EPISODE SUMMARY

At approximately 9:45 a.m. Ms. Anderson stood in front of the room and began the lesson saying, "Now, does everyone remember what we were talking about yesterday?" One or two students responded. She restated the responses saying, "Yes. The election of 1824...and the election of 1828...Who was elected President in the election of 1824?" Several students responded. Ms. Anderson restated their response saying, "John Buchanan. Good... What about 1832?" Several students called out, "Andrew Jackson." Ms. Anderson restated their answer saying, "Andrew Jackson. Good. We spent time talking about Jackson and his...and what a good President he was and stuff like that...Today, we are going to look at an important issue...It has something to do with what we talked about yesterday...the Tariff of Abomination."

Ms. Anderson then moved into the middle of the lesson by asking, "Can anybody tell me what the tariff was?" Several students spoke out a response. She called on a particular student and he answered saying, "Yes, it was a bill that...kinda backfired on them...." Ms. Anderson reinforced the student's response by saying, "Right. It is very high. It increased the price of the goods a lot...Well, a lot of people in the country opposed this tariff...." During this discussion, Ms. Anderson went to the board and wrote the words, *Tariff of Abomination*. Underneath that title she wrote the word, *Reasons.* When she had written this outline she stated, "The first thing we are going to discuss...is the reasons the South opposed the tariff...OK." As the discussion continued, Ms. Anderson gave a reason for the tariff, explained it to the students, and then wrote each reason on the board. As she did this, the students took notes.

When this information had been presented, Ms. Anderson moved the discussion to the topic of South Carolina seceding from the Union, saying, "Another influential protest in South Carolina came from John C. Calhoun. Do you all remember that name? Can anyone tell me anything about him?" A few students responded. Ms. Anderson then began to tell them about this individual. She concluded her summary about John C. Calhoun by saying, "I want you to know that name." She erased the board and wrote *John C. Calhoun*. Underneath she highlighted two facts about him: *Wrote the Exposition and Protest of South Carolina and Protest of Tariff of 1828.*

At 10:00 Ms. Anderson turned on the overhead projector and stated, "OK. Like I said this is important. You need to get it all down...'Cause it's very important." She continued the discussion by revealing each point with a shadow sheet. The students took notes as she elaborated on each point. After the discussion of each point, she stated, "Now what we're going to do now is I'm going to divide you up into groups of three. And there's three questions I want the groups to look at. I'll write them down while you finish taking the notes off the transparency." Ms. Anderson went to the board and began writing the three questions she wanted the groups to discuss. At 10:05 she asked, "Is everybody finishing up?...We have twenty people so we should have five groups of four and in your groups I want you to answer each of the following three questions...You can use the overhead... your notes...your textbook to help you do this. I want you to tell me three reasons why South Carolina should have the right to nullify the tariff and secede from the Union. Then I want you to come up with three reasons why they shouldn't have been able to nullify the tariff and secede from the Union. Then you as a group decide what is right...." One student asked, " Do we have to write it down?" Ms. Anderson responded, "You need to have one person write down your answers...I'm going to give you about ten minutes to come with your answers."

The students began selecting group members and moving into groups at 10:06. The students worked in groups until 10:20 when Ms. Anderson inquired, "Is everybody finished? OK. Let's get back to South Carolina...What group wants to be first? Do I have a volunteer?" Students talked out. Ms. Anderson called upon a student to read. Each group reported back answers to the questions. Ms. Anderson responded to students by saying such things as, " OK. Good," "Do you have anything more?" "OK. Good. Sounds like you all understand."

The lesson concluded when Ms. Anderson stated, "You need to see both sides of the situation. When you all did your projects, did you have to look at both pros and cons of the issue?" The students responded by telling her about their projects. When they got too loud she said, "OK. I can't understand one person. You're too loud." The students stopped talking out. She then continued, saying, "I just want you to be able to look at both sides of a situation...In the end South Carolina thought they had made Congress back down...and the Union thought....Was that the case? In other words...there was no resolution...It remained an open sore.... That's it for today. Everybody remember that chapter nine is due tomorrow." Students began talking and moving toward the exit.

TEACHING PERFORMANCE

PROFESSIONAL/INTERPERSONAL/ LEADERSHIP COMPETENCIES

1. Demonstrates Initiative for Assuming Responsibility. Ms. Anderson began teaching classes during the second week of her student teaching experience. Her projected long-range plan shows an increase in this responsibility each week. Ms. Anderson described as a strength on her first weekly conference report her "eagerness to begin teaching."

2. Demonstrates Self-Assurance. Ms. Anderson appears confident and poised in front of students. She moved easily across the front of the room as she presented the lecture; she looked directly at the students and responded to their questions confidently and without any hesitation.

3. Works Well with Colleagues. Her supervising teacher indicated that Ms. Anderson is very cooperative and follows through on tasks assigned. For example, on the most recent weekly conference report, the cooperating teacher wrote, "Nicki did a super job this week. She prepared the class well for an upcoming class test."

PLANNING/RECORD KEEPING/ ORGANIZATIONAL COMPETENCIES

1. Documents Self-Evaluation of Each Lesson Taught. Ms. Anderson has started a field notebook which contains information on the following areas:

- Daily journal of reflections
- Long-range plan for 10-week period
- Weekly and daily lesson plans

2. Meets Planning Deadlines. Ms. Anderson has submitted the required forms documenting her student teaching progress each week. She has met all current planning deadlines.

Classroom Performance Competencies

1. Creates Positive Learning Environment. Ms. Anderson supports students by providing encouragement and dignifying academic responses. She conducted the class in a businesslike manner. She asked routine questions during the lecture with average student participation. Student-teacher rapport was good.

2. Demonstrates Acceptable Written and Oral Expression. Ms. Anderson has a well-modulated voice which can be easily heard. She used her voice effectively through word emphasis, pauses, and varying her volume. Her grammar was generally acceptable but occasionally she used informal expressions, verbal interupters (OK) and awkward grammatical structure. On her self-assessment of a videotaped lesson she wrote, "I also see a lot of personal improvements I need to make: my Southern accent, using my hands too much, and using better grammar." No written communication errors were noted on any lesson plans or board notes.

3. Competence in Teaching Field. Ms. Anderson demonstrated adequate knowledge of the content presented. She presented the lesson as organized per her course objectives and procedures. The lesson reflected a clear beginning, middle, and end.

4. Uses Several Instructional Methods Appropriately. Ms. Anderson demonstrated two instructional methods: class lecture and small group work. The lecture had a clear organization and sequence. Ms. Anderson used the blackboard and the overhead to show this organization; she also repeated key points and summarized them. After the lecture the students worked in small groups to develop responses to three questions posed by the teacher. All groups then presented their thoughts on each question to the entire class.

5. Manages Disruptive/Off-Task Behavior. Students generally were on task and followed directions. Distractions that occurred did not interfere with the instructional environment. Ms. Anderson verbally reminded students of expected behavior and they responded. She used low-level intervention strategies to redirect three students who were off task; she monitored their behavior until they remained on task through proximity and scanning.

POST-OBSERVATION SUMMARY AND REFLECTIONS

1. Facilitates Student Learning. Research on effective teaching points out the benefit of varying the learning activities. Cooperative learning or collaborative learning is an effective technique of subgrouping. How can you utilize this technique more effectively? What procedures can you put into place to help groups get organized more quickly? What products do you want the groups to generate? How will you monitor the productivity of individuals within the groups?

2. Maintains Learner Involvement in Instruction. Questioning is a skill that teachers need to develop, and research on effective teaching suggests the following tips:

- Questions should be planned and written into the lesson plan.
- Questions should reflect both lower and higher levels of cognitive thinking.
- Teacher should address a question to entire group, provide wait time, and then call on a volunteer or non-volunteer.

What procedures have you planned for conducting question-and-answer parts of your lesson?

Please review this report and think about the questions raised. We will meet tomorrow during your planning period to discuss your lesson.

Summary

"If you always do what you've always done,
you'll always be what you've always been."
Wycoff, 1991, p. 87

Writing effective memos, letters and reports is well within your reach. The secret to success is breaking "writing" resistance. Avoiding your in-basket because you find it time-consuming, overwhelming, and stressful means you haven't developed a strategic game plan to face the challenge head on. You can either develop a plan to handle your writing tasks or you can continue to drift from item to item unfocused and unarmed. In order to survive on the job, you need to develop a writing plan that includes attending to the key points raised in this chapter and in the text. Start with the notion that effective writing is possible and critical to your success as a school leader. Eliminate all the excuses that say you don't have enough time, enough skill, enough energy. If you really want to write well, you will find the time, the skill, and the energy. ATTACK!

Resources

Books And Articles

Title: *Persuasive Writing: Communicating Effectively in Business*
Author: Herman Holtz
Publisher: McGraw-Hill, 1983

The author centers on techniques of persuading people through proposals, brochures, reports, speeches, letters, memos, and newsletters.

Title: *The Perfect Memo and the Perfect Letter*
Author: Patricia Westheimer
Publisher: Scott, Foresman and Co., 1990

Both of these books provide quick methods for breaking writing into manageable steps, instructions for organizing, and tips to overcome writer's block. Using "before" and "after" writing samples, the author shows how to improve correspondence. The author also includes a brief guide to grammar, punctuation, and spelling as well as a wide variety of memo and letter formats.

Title: *Written Communications and the School Administrator*
Author: Audrey Joyce
Publisher: Allyn and Bacon, 1991

No matter what the situation, good or bad, as an administrator you've got to write well. The author gives practical writing instruction in an easy-to-grasp way. The book contains over 100 sample letters arranged by purpose and audience.

Title: *School Administrator's Complete Letter Book*
Author: Gerald Tomlinson,
Publisher: Prentice Hall, 1984

More than 100 memos and letters written to parents, teachers, students, other school administrators, business people, and the community at large. This resource guide deals with issues faced by school principals and the types of writing demanded on the job. Each writing document responds to a specific need in a courteous, thoughtful, and professional manner.

SEMINARS AND WORKSHOPS

The workshops and seminars listed in this guide were chosen for their appeal to school administrators. Since the publication of this text, some seminars may have been upgraded or replaced and others may no longer be offered. Similarly, costs and locations may have also changed. We recommend that you contact the consulting group directly for current information and availability.

Title: *How to Sharpen Your Business Writing Skills*
Consulting Group: American Management Association
Contact Number: Tel: 518-891-0065

A writing program for professionals whose job requires written communications. Program focuses on how to write like you speak, how to grab the reader's attention, and how to organize your writing documents.

Title: *From the Desk of… A Written Communication Program for School Administrators*
Consulting Group: National Association of Secondary School Principals
Contact Number: Tel: 703-860-0200

A developmental program that engages participants in multiple writing tasks based on the job demands in the principalship.

Instructional techniques focus on how to get started, organizing your writing, assessing your audiences, sharpening word choice, and producing high-quality documents.

Title: *Effective Reports, Proposals, and Memos*
Consulting Group: Information Mapping, Inc.
Contact Number: Tel: 617-890-7003

Outlining the key concepts of the information mapping method, this program highlights techniques for organizing information, refining your content, and applying the practiced strategies on the job.

CHAPTER REFERENCES

Forbes, M. (1979). How to write a business letter. In Golen, Figgins, and Smeltzer (Eds.), *Business communication* (pp. 78-81). New York: John Wiley & Sons.

Golen, S. & Ellzey, G. (1984). Communicating with graphics: A picture can be worth a thousand words. In Golen, Figgins, and Smeltzer (Eds.), *Business communication* (pp. 109-115). New York: John Wiley & Sons.

Hennington, J. (1978) Memorandums—an effective communication tool for managers. In Golen, Figgins, and Smeltzer (Eds.), *Business communication* (pp. 82-89). New York: John Wiley & Sons.

Tomlinson, G. (1984). School administrator's complete letter book. Englewood Cliffs, NJ: Prentice Hall, Inc.

Vinci, V. (1975), Ten report writing pitfalls: How to avoid them In Golen, Figgins, and Smeltzer (Eds.), *Business communication* (pp. 102-108). New York: John Wiley & Sons.

Yerkes, D., & Morgan S., (1991). *Strategies for success: An administrator's guide to writing.* Reston, VA: National Association for Secondary School Principals.

Wakin, E. (1982). Better business writing. In Golen, Figgins, and Smeltzer (Eds.), *Business communication* (pp. 99-100). New York: John Wiley & Sons.

Wycoff, J. (1991). *Mindmapping*. New York: Berkley Books.

Note to the Reader

If you enjoyed this book, we recommend you contact Eye On Education to purchase a copy of *Disk with Workbook to Accompany Written Expression: The Principal's Survival Guide* (ISBN 1-883001-42-0). It provides principals with the tools they need to put into practice the concepts outlined in this book. The workbook expands the topics covered here and provides additional examples.

On the diskette you will find many of the sample documents printed in both this book and the workbook. You may use these documents as templates for your own writing tasks.